JACK THORNE

Jack Thorne's plays for the stage in
War with the Wireless (Donmar Warehouse, London, 2023); an
adaptation of Hirokazu Kore-eda's film *After Life* (National
Theatre, London, 2021); *Harry Potter and the Cursed Child*
(Palace Theatre, London, since 2016, and Lyric Theatre, New
York, since 2018; winner of the 2017 Olivier Award for Best New
Play and the 2018 Tony Award for Best Play); a reimagining of
A Christmas Carol by Charles Dickens (Old Vic Theatre, 2017,
2018, 2019); *the end of history…* (Royal Court Theatre, 2019);
a musical adaptation of *King Kong* (Broadway Theatre, New
York, 2018); a new version of Georg Büchner's *Woyzeck* (Old Vic
Theatre, 2017); *Junkyard* (Headlong/Bristol Old Vic/Rose Theatre
Kingston/Theatr Clwyd, 2017); *The Solid Life of Sugar Water*
(Graeae Theatre Company); *Hope* (Royal Court Theatre, London,
2014); adaptations of *Let the Right One In* (National Theatre of
Scotland at Dundee Rep, the Royal Court and the Apollo Theatre,
London, 2013/14) and *Stuart: A Life Backwards* (Underbelly,
Edinburgh, and tour, 2013); *Mydidae* (Soho, 2012; Trafalgar
Studios, 2013); an adaptation of Friedrich Dürrenmatt's *The
Physicists* (Donmar Warehouse, 2012); *Bunny* (Underbelly,
Edinburgh, 2010; Soho, 2011); *2nd May 1997* (Bush, 2009);
Burying Your Brother in the Pavement (National Theatre
Connections, 2008); *When You Cure Me* (Bush, 2005; Radio 3's
Drama on Three, 2006); *Fanny and Faggot* (Pleasance,
Edinburgh, 2004 and 2007; Finborough, 2007; English Theatre of
Bruges, 2007; Trafalgar Studios, 2007); and *Stacy* (Tron, 2006;
Arcola, 2007; Trafalgar Studios, 2007).

His radio plays include *Left at the Angel* (Radio 4, 2007), an
adaptation of *The Hunchback of Notre Dame* (2009), and an
original play *People Snogging in Public Places* (Radio 3's Wire
slot, 2009).

For television, Jack has five BAFTAs for his work on *National
Treasure* (Best Mini-Series, 2017); *This is England '90* (Best
Mini-Series, 2016); *Don't Take My Baby* (Best Single Drama,
2016); *The Fades* (Best Drama Series, 2012); *This is England '88*
(Best Mini-Series, 2012). He is also the recipient of an
International Emmy Award for *Help* (Best TV Movie/Mini-Series).

His other writing for television includes *Then Barbara Met Alan*, the BBC adaptation of Philip Pullman's *His Dark Materials*, *CripTales*, *The Eddy*, *The Accident*, *The Virtues*, *Kiri*, *Electric Dreams*, *The Last Panthers*, *Glue*, *Shameless*, *Skins* and *Cast-Offs*.

In 2022 Jack was the recipient of both the Writers' Guild of Great Britain award for Outstanding Contribution to Writing, and the Royal Television Society's award for Outstanding Contribution to British Television, and in 2023 the National Film and Television School awarded Jack their honorary fellowship.

His work for film includes the features *Enola Holmes 1* and *2*, *The Secret Garden*, *Radioactive*, *Dirt Music*, *Wonder*, *War Book*, *A Long Way Down* and *The Scouting Book for Boys*.

Jack is a patron of Graeae Theatre Company, an associate artist of The Old Vic, and a fellow of the Royal Society of Literature. He is a founding member of the pressure group Underlying Health Condition.

Jack Thorne

THE MOTIVE
AND THE CUE

NICK HERN BOOKS

London

www.nickhernbooks.co.uk

A Nick Hern Book

The Motive and the Cue first published as a paperback original in Great Britain in 2023 by Nick Hern Books Limited, The Glasshouse, 49a Goldhawk Road, London W12 8QP

The Motive and the Cue copyright © 2023 Jack Thorne

Jack Thorne has asserted his right to be identified as the author of this work

Cover image: Richard Burton and John Gielgud conferring during rehearsals for the stage production of *Hamlet*, photo by Leo Friedman, 1964 © NYPL
Art direction and design by National Theatre Graphic Design Studio

Designed and typeset by Nick Hern Books, London
Printed in Great Britain by Mimeo Ltd, Huntingdon, Cambridgeshire PE29 6XX

A CIP catalogue record for this book is available from the British Library

ISBN   978 1 83904 153 2

The Motive and the Cue was first performed in the Lyttelton auditorium of the National Theatre, London, on 2 May 2023 (previews from 20 April). The cast was as follows:

DILLON EVANS (*Osric*)	Aaron Anthony
MICK BURROWS (*Stage Manager*)	Tom Babbage
HUME CRONYN (*Polonius*)	Allan Corduner
EILEEN HERLIE (*Gertrude*)	Janie Dee
SUSANNAH MASON (*Stage Manager*)	Elena Delia
GEORGE VOSKOVEC (*Player King*)	Ryan Ellsworth
RICHARD BURTON (*Hamlet*)	Johnny Flynn
SIR JOHN GIELGUD (*Director and Ghost*)	Mark Gatiss
LINDA MARSH (*Ophelia*)	Phoebe Horn
JESSICA LEVY (*assistant to Sir John*)	Aysha Kala
ELIZABETH TAYLOR (*a world apart*)	Tuppence Middleton
WILLIAM REDFIELD (*Guildenstern*)	Luke Norris
FREDERICK YOUNG (*Barnardo*)	Huw Parmenter
CLEMENT FOWLER (*Rosencrantz*)	David Ricardo-Pearce
ALFRED DRAKE (*Claudius*)	David Tarkenter
CHRISTINE COOPER (*Player Queen*)	Kate Tydman
HUGH McHAFFIE (*a further world apart*)	Laurence Ubong Williams
ROBERT MILLI (*Horatio*)	Michael Walters

All other parts to be played by members of the company.

Director	Sam Mendes
Set Designer	Es Devlin
Costume Designer	Katrina Lindsay
Lighting Designer	Jon Clark
Composer	Benjamin Kwasi Burrell
Sound Designer	Paul Arditti
Casting	Alastair Coomer CDG and Naomi Downham
Associate Director	Zoé Ford Burnett
Associate Set Designer	Amalie White
Dialect Coach	Charmian Hoare
Company Voice Work	Cathleen McCarron
Staff Director	Yasmin Hafesji

The Motive and the Cue is inspired by *Letters from an Actor* by William Redfield and *John Gielgud Directs Richard Burton in Hamlet* by Richard L. Sterne.

Acknowledgements

Sam Mendes, Es Devlin, Rufus Norris, Caro Newling, Rachel Quinney, Clint Dyer, Nina Steiger, Sarah Clarke, William Redfield, Adam Redfield, David Rothberg, Richard Sterne, Rachel Taylor, Rachel Mason, Helena Clark, Stuart Tubby and Mariella Johnson.

J.T.

For Buzz,
who taught me bravery this year

Characters

RICHARD BURTON, *Hamlet*
ROBERT MILLI, *Horatio*
HUME CRONYN, *Polonius*
EILEEN HERLIE, *Gertrude*
LINDA MARSH, *Ophelia*
WILLIAM REDFIELD, *Guildenstern*
CLEMENT FOWLER, *Rosencrantz*
GEORGE VOSKOVEC, *Player King*
FREDERICK YOUNG, *Barnardo*
ALFRED DRAKE, *Claudius*
CHRISTINE COOPER, *Player Queen*
DILLON EVANS, *Osric*
SIR JOHN GIELGUD, *director and Ghost*
JESSICA LEVY, *assistant to Sir John*
SUSANNAH MASON, *stage manager*
MICK BURROWS, *stage manager*
ELIZABETH TAYLOR, *a world apart*
HUGH McHAFFIE, *a further world apart*

This text went to press before the end of rehearsals and so may differ slightly from the play as performed.

ACT ONE: THE MOTIVE

Scene One

Day One – 'How Came He Mad?'

A rehearsal room. It's 1964. Table and chairs are laid out. The actors are around them and upon them.

Applause from the assembled company, as GIELGUD *stands with a distinguished air.*

GIELGUD. Please. Good gracious. Not necessary. It is a joy to see you all here. Wonderful in fact. Before we read, perhaps a few words…

CRONYN. We're reading now?

GIELGUD. If you don't mind indulging me.

CRONYN. I think many of us thought we would read tomorrow.

DRAKE. I thought so too.

GIELGUD. I apologise. You were expecting small talk. Yes, it is nice to flirt a little before we get entirely into bed. What should we discuss?

CRONYN. No. We don't need to – curate discussion…

HERLIE. I've plenty to say about those jackals outside. I was not dressed appropriately for pictures –

CRONYN. I was in corduroy.

HERLIE. – and told them so, but it did not stop them.

CRONYN. Corduroy.

BURTON. Eileen, I'm sorry, they're entirely my mess, I should have forewarned you. Nonsense, all of it. I do so hate it.

HERLIE. It was – tiresome –

GIELGUD. 'Reputation is an idle and most false imposition' –
so hard for you, Dick, such rabidity, but I suppose they may
help ticket sales. I took – stage door of course.

Beat. That stops things. He looks around the room.

It's possibly easier to keep things a little formal. Shall I be
mother? Does everyone have the coffee they need? Is there
cake? We should have had cake. Breaking bread together I'm
not such a fan of, but breaking cake seems altogether better.
We won't go around the room because everyone forgets the
non-famous names and knows already the famous ones. But
one name I would like to celebrate, this is Jessica, she's
assisting me, she's delightful.

JESSICA. Hello. Next time I'll bring cake.

GIELGUD. You see? Before we read, a few things I thought I'd
say…

He consults notes, he's nervous.

Some of you may ask: Why a 'rehearsal' production? Why
not merely modern dress?

I think this: Like all of you, I have so often seen a final
run-through, before the costumes and sets arrive, which had
drive and simplicity and… oh, an ease, somehow –

REDFIELD *enters the room, surreptitiously. He looks over
and sees that everyone's gathered.*

– which the actors never got back once the stone columns
and marble tables came on and all the yards and yards of red
velvet and blue silk and ruffs and farthingales were tossed
about their simple bodies.

BURTON. Some bodies aren't that simple.

There's laughter. REDFIELD *takes off his coat and then
lingers – unwilling to disrupt any further.*

GIELGUD. So much for traditional productions. (*Without looking
at him.*) William, as enjoyable as your well-timed entrance is,
the agony is beginning to infect us all. Please do sit.

REDFIELD. I'm so sorry. I was caught out by – I'm sorry.

JESSICA *brings him a script, which he takes gratefully.*

GIELGUD. Yes, you must be. Now, where was I? Ah yes. Very well, then, why not contemporary clothing and drawing-room sets? Because it's even more depressing really, and I've seen so much of it.

There's more laughter, GIELGUD *enjoys it, he's warming up.*

Claudius drinks a dreary martini, and Rosencrantz and Guildenstern enter with frightfully tight – umbrellas –

There's laughter.

– and Laertes offers Ophelia a Lucky Strike from a gold cigarette case and they both puff away while Polonius talks of the French...

There's much laughter.

Richard and I have discussed this endlessly –

BURTON. Endlessly –

There's laughter.

GIELGUD. Oh dear boy, and we finally wondered if it wouldn't be a neat trick to do it as a run-through. As few props and gimmicks as possible. A pre-dress-rehearsal run-through of a traditional production put on just before the sets have been erected and the costumes fitted. We will all have to be careful of what we wear, but I have so often been fascinated by what actors wear to rehearsals. Have you noticed that what an actor wears on the first day usually indicates how he feels about his part? One even gets a hint of how he feels about himself.

He looks around the room.

Some are confident, some are less confident, some are ready to have confidence thrust upon them.

BURTON *stands up and lights a cigarette.*

And some think they're still in their library at home.

BURTON *nods with a grin. There's a scatter of laughter.*

Granville-Barker used to say that *Hamlet* was a permanent rehearsal, and I believe that. I would like you to wear what you would normally wear to rehearsals, and sooner or later we'll all hit upon something. I think it could work out quite well. Don't you?

There's applause.

Good. Now we may read –

BURTON. May I first – say a little –

GIELGUD *looks up, surprised.*

GIELGUD. It is your stage.

BURTON. Welcome. As I say, I'm sorry for the – fireworks outside. Should die down in a day or two. It's my responsibility not yours. I hold myself accountable for everything but Hume's corduroy.

Laughter.

Reputation is a… What's the line, Sir John?

GIELGUD. Ignore me.

BURTON. But I just wanted to say how excited I am to be here, amongst you, and how excited I am to have this wonderful man directing us.

GIELGUD. Oh, if you're going to stick flowers up my bum you are not allowed to speak –

There's laughter.

BURTON. Here is a theatrical gentleman in possession of a conviction. And that conviction is the Actor. First and foremost, eternally and always, when it comes to the theatre, the actor. Oh, yes, 'The play's the thing!' but – we all know – the playwright is not an integer.

HERLIE. Amen.

BURTON. If a group of primitive men sit around in a cave, can a playwright entertain them? Not unless he's a singer, juggler, tight-rope walker, dancer –

GIELGUD. Stripper.

There's laughter.

BURTON. We are the bullfighters. And this man knows it. He wishes to unleash our skills and put them to Shakespeare's use. He aims for swiftness, lucidity and a clean, sharp line. We are *stripping* back the stage, so he can show your worth. Now an actor cannot change during a twenty-five-day rehearsal, nor can any director bestow or bless an actor with more talent –

CRONYN. One can only hope –

There's laughter.

BURTON. – but a director can memorise an actor, he can identify with him and bring the best from him. Such an approach takes sympathy and faith. That is what we will make, a new *Hamlet* for our time, held on our shoulders. Together we share the responsibility for what theatre can be – Sir John will unleash it in us – let us rise to his challenge.

There's even harder applause.

BURTON *sits, the joust has begun.*

GIELGUD. What wonderful kind words. Quite quite unnecessary. Right. Act One. Scene One. Elsinore. A platform before the castle. Francisco is at his post, Barnardo enters…

The actors settle, open their texts.

BARNARDO.
Who's there…

FRANCISCO.
Nay, answer me: stand, and unfold yourself…

BARNARDO.
Long live the King!

Scene Two

Day One – 'The Time Invites You'

We are inside the rooms of Elizabeth Taylor and Richard Burton, with REDFIELD, TAYLOR *and* BURTON. *She is effortlessly draped over him.*

REDFIELD. I won't. Thank you.

TAYLOR. 'I won't. Thank you.' Listen to him, all sombre like an actor. You must.

REDFIELD. I don't drink champagne. The bubbles don't agree with me.

BURTON. I'm the same, old man. Gives me the farts all night long, does that stop me – ?

TAYLOR. It really doesn't. Dick once challenged me to a blowing-wind competition and his range was quite extraordinary…

BURTON. She played her part.

TAYLOR. What'll you be?

REDFIELD. Oh. Whatever you have.

BURTON. We have everything.

    REDFIELD *is shy and embarrassed.*

REDFIELD. Beefeater martini?

TAYLOR. Stirred or shaken?

REDFIELD. Shaken.

TAYLOR. A gentleman. No less. An olive? A lemon?

REDFIELD. You really mustn't…

TAYLOR. I simply must. We have olives and lemons.

REDFIELD. No olives. No lemons.

BURTON (*sung*).
    Olives and lemons said the bells of St Clements,
    I'm pissed as a newt, said the bells of St Flute.

    TAYLOR *waits for* BURTON *to finish.*

TAYLOR. Frozen glass?

REDFIELD. Please.

She exits. BURTON *and* REDFIELD *are left.*

BURTON. She does that. She likes to serve. Gives her –
something. I can't abide it myself. Less of a novelty for me
I suspect.

Beat. REDFIELD *looks after her and to the door.*

The others will be here soon.

REDFIELD. Will Sir John come?

BURTON. He was invited.

REDFIELD *nods.*

How do you think the old stick is getting on?

REDFIELD. The read-through was very fast.

BURTON. Wasn't it just?

REDFIELD. And Sir John seemed delighted by it. The speed,
I mean…

BURTON. And little else? I thought the same. Though he
laughed at your bits.

He drinks.

Quite right, of course, one mustn't feed an actor's ego too
soon, otherwise it may get bloated and ill.

REDFIELD. I thought you read the part –

BURTON. I insist on you not giving me a review yet.

REDFIELD. But just to say –

BURTON. No.

Beat.

He's quite right about the other thing too – speed is
everything.

REDFIELD. With *Hamlet* (I always find) –

BURTON. When Peter played it – O'Toole I mean – at The Old
Vic, they did the full text. The trouble is a Londoner without
a private car has to catch the eleven-twenty Underground or
he'll spend the night with friends. Apparently 'goodnight,
sweet Prince' was not a farewell to dying Hamlet but a sad
bye-bye to departing patrons.

REDFIELD (*laughing*). Shakespeare didn't consider the
subway, clearly.

BURTON. You know, we tossed a coin, he and I, as to who
would play the Dane in London and who in New York. I won't
tell you who won.

REDFIELD. And did you do the same over choice of director?

BURTON. He got Larry, he was playing the National. I –
Gielgud felt better for this.

Beat.

Larry is too similar to me in any case. Though I thought
Peter would have done better without him too – he casts
a long shadow –

REDFIELD. And Sir John doesn't?

BURTON. His shadow is different, though he wouldn't like me
saying so.

Beat.

I grew up on Sir John, you know. His records, his writings,
and the stories my father told me about his acting. Saw him
for the first time when I was twelve. My father loved him.
I loved him.

REDFIELD. Lee Strasberg said to me once: 'When Gielgud
speaks the verse, I can hear Shakespeare thinking.'

BURTON. You're part of Lee's crowd, are you? Makes sense.

TAYLOR *re-enters*.

TAYLOR. You know who taught me the method? Mickey
Rooney. When we were shooting *National Velvet* I had to cry
for a scene and he told me – 'You should think that your

father is dying and your mother has to wash clothes for
a living, and your little brother is out selling newspapers.'
Well, I did and it worked. Your glass.

She hands it to REDFIELD.

REDFIELD. Thank you. I loved that movie.

TAYLOR *re-sits on* BURTON. *There's a ring at the door.*

TAYLOR. And yet I suspect Lee Strasberg and Mickey Rooney
would *not* get on.

BURTON. Darling, you're oversimplifying.

TAYLOR. Really? Tell me how.

BURTON. Hume!

It's CRONYN. *He enters theatrically.*

CRONYN. Debauchery already? Will someone please put their
clothes on.

TAYLOR. I wish we were naked. Hello, Hume.

CRONYN. Darling.

BURTON. Did they accost you on the way in?

CRONYN. I haven't been accosted since 1955, and I'm sure
that was merely an accident.

There's a ring at the door.

TAYLOR. How's Jessica?

CRONYN. Angry with me, for being where she isn't.

TAYLOR. I'm sure she's just trying to mask how delighted she
is. Champagne?

CRONYN. And why not?

BURTON. Ah. Here's Eileen now.

HERLIE enters.

TAYLOR. This must be the great Eileen Herlie.

CRONYN. Not sure 'great' is the correct adjective.

HERLIE. I know you love me, Hume. (*To* TAYLOR.) Enchanted.

TAYLOR. As am I. Please – (*Indicates glass.*)

> MILLI *and* MARSH *follow* HERLIE *in.*

BURTON. And Milli – and Linda. All my favourite people all together.

TAYLOR. Then they are now all my favourite people too. Robert Milli, am I right?

MILLI. You are. It's an honour.

TAYLOR. Do take a glass. And you must be –

MARSH. Linda.

BURTON. William here was asking about Olivier. If you've a question about how Olivier would have done our *Hamlet* – you should ask Eileen…

REDFIELD. I wasn't – technically – asking –

HERLIE. Come come.

BURTON. He suckled upon her.

HERLIE. He did no such thing.

BURTON. You were his Gertrude.

HERLIE. Yes.

MARSH. I loved that film.

REDFIELD. Me too.

BURTON. And how much younger than him are you, Mother?

HERLIE. A mere eleven years. But need I remind you I'm only seven years older than you.

> *There's applause.*

CRONYN. Ouch.

BURTON. Science must have been different then. We're almost out of champagne-guzzlers. Come through and I'll show you the bedroom of the famous Elizabeth Taylor.

TAYLOR. Dick!

BURTON. Lizzie. Come on now.

TAYLOR (*enjoyably supplicant*). If you see knickers they're his not mine.

BURTON. Good girl. Adventurers, follow me.

CRONYN. I won't say no, this place is a palace.

> BURTON *leads them through.* TAYLOR *and* REDFIELD *are left alone.*

> *Beat. She realises* REDFIELD *is staying.*

TAYLOR. You don't want to see my bedroom?

REDFIELD. I wouldn't like anyone to see mine.

TAYLOR. Then we're quite, quite different.

REDFIELD. Are we?

TAYLOR. I'm sure I know you.

> REDFIELD *is unsure how to deal with this quiet time.*

REDFIELD. We have some – mutual friends – Joan Lorring, Roddy McDowall, Montgomery Clift.

TAYLOR. Oh. That's a list. Were you a child actor too?

REDFIELD. Yes.

TAYLOR. But not in films?

REDFIELD. Mostly theatre.

TAYLOR. How delightful.

> REDFIELD *looks longingly towards the door the others left by.*

> You're an outsider, aren't you? Like me. Drink up. You'll feel better soon.

REDFIELD. It's a very – tasty – Beefeater.

TAYLOR. I'm sure. Now, tell me, it's a good company. He says.

REDFIELD. Yes.

TAYLOR. Leading actors playing lesser roles, just to be part of it.

REDFIELD. That's how it was sold to me.

TAYLOR. I'm desperate to come to rehearsals but he's being beastly and won't let me.

REDFIELD. That seems a shame, as you're here.

TAYLOR. On my honeymoon no less. Stuck in a room while the press amass below. Rapunzel in a tower of dirty newspaper. He says he'll keep throwing these parties for me. As a solace. But I want to be in the room. He says I won't understand. He says that it's different from film – an actor must be willing to look silly or insane.

REDFIELD. True enough.

TAYLOR. Would I ruin things? If I were there to see it? I'd rather die than irritate anyone or disturb their way of working. But I do want to learn, and I like silliness and insanity.

REDFIELD. If it were in my gift, you'd be in there in a second.

TAYLOR. How kind. Oh look. Your frozen glass. It's no longer frozen.

The gang come back from the tour.

BURTON. Linda has decided to move in.

MARSH. They're beautiful rooms.

BURTON. Royal rooms for royal people. What do you think, honey? Could we have Linda live on the couch? A concubine for our times.

MARSH. Is that what I'll be?

TAYLOR. If she's free and available she might be fun to play with.

CRONYN. Perhaps we could rotate it. I always thought I'd give good concubine.

VOSKOVEC *enters, with* DRAKE.

HERLIE. Disastrous casting.

VOSKOVEC. Is this right? The doorman ushered us through.

TAYLOR. This is right. And you're welcome. Elizabeth.

She extends a hand.

VOSKOVEC. I – know.

He shakes her hand.

CRONYN. Tell her your name, George.

VOSKOVEC. George.

TAYLOR. Charmed. To meet you both.

DRAKE. Well, I need to talk to my agent. My digs are nothing like this.

TAYLOR Then drink up and pretend they are.

There's laughter. FOWLER, YOUNG, COOPER *and* EVANS *enter.*

BURTON. Ah, here we are. Finally. Come in. Come in.

BURTON *stands on a chair. He dings a glass.*

Now we are all together, I must say a few words…

MILLI. No.

BURTON. It is my position as host to make a –

TAYLOR. I'm the host, darling, and everyone has clearly had enough of you.

CRONYN. No more bloody speeches. Grab him.

BURTON. No.

CRONYN (*to the young cast*). Why be young if you can't lift a man?

BURTON *is lifted, laughing, off the chair.*

BURTON. DAMN you! Damn you all! Damn you!

TAYLOR. DON'T HARM HIM. Or rather do. Do whatever you want to him.

They start throwing him up and down.

BURTON. Oh Jesus. Mother. Mother. Save me.

HERLIE. No need for another speech.

BURTON. You're all arseholes of the highest order. You'll do my back in, then where will you be?

CRONYN. One Prince short.

MILLI *and* CRONYN *and then all.*
For he's a jolly good fellow,
For he's a jolly good fellow,
For he's a jolly good fellow,
And so say all of us.

TAYLOR. He's not a good fellow. He's a bloody awful fellow.

Scene Three

Day Four – 'Mark Me'

BURTON *and* MILLI *stand together, Hamlet and Horatio now.*

BURTON.
The air bites shrewdly; it is very cold.

MILLI.
It is a nipping and an eager air.

BURTON.
What hour now?

MILLI.
I think it lacks of twelve.

BURTON.
No, it is struck.

MILLI.
Indeed? I heard it not. It then draws near the season
Wherein the spirit held his wont to walk.

BURTON. Cue trumpets.

MILLI.

What does this mean, my Lord?

BURTON.

The King doth wake tonight and takes his rouse,
Keeps wassail, and the swaggering upspring reels,
And, as he drains his draughts of Rhenish down,
The kettledrum and trumpet thus bray out
The triumph of his pledge.

MILLI.

Is it a custom?

BURTON.

Ay, marry, is't.
But to my mind, though I am native here
And to the manner born, it is a custom
More honoured in the breach than the observance.
This heavy-headed revel east and west
Makes us traduced and taxed of other nations.

Sorry. Sorry. I've lost my place.

GIELGUD.

'They clepe us drunkards and with swinish phrase' –

BURTON.

Soil our addition.

It's disconcerting you don't need a prompter.

Makes us traduced and taxed of other nations... Blah blah
blah.

Doth all the noble substance of a doubt
To his own scandal.

GIELGUD. Never has 'blah blah blah' sounded more
Shakespearean. You're right. It needs cuts. I'll get them done
for the next pass. Jessica –

JESSICA. Noted.

GIELGUD. 'Look, my Lord'...

MILLI.

Look, my Lord, it comes!

GIELGUD. Enter Ghost. New lighting state. Please don't skip through this piece.

BURTON.

Angels and ministers of grace defend us!
Be thou a spirit of health or goblin damned,
Bring with thee airs from heaven or blasts from hell,
Be thy intents wicked or charitable,
Thou com'st in such a questionable shape
That I will speak to thee. I'll call thee Hamlet,
King, father, royal Dane. O, answer me!
Let me not burst in ignorance; but tell
Why thy canonized bones, hearsèd in death,
Have burst their cerements; why the sepulchre
Wherein we saw thee quietly interred,
Hath oped his ponderous and marble jaws
To cast thee up again. What may this mean,
That thou, dead corse, again in complete steel
Revisits thus the glimpses of the moon,
Making night hideous, and we fools of nature
So horridly to shake our disposition
With thoughts beyond the reaches of our souls?
Say, why is this? Wherefore? What should we do?

GIELGUD. The Ghost beckons Hamlet.

BURTON *plays it beautifully.*

MILLI.

It beckons you to go away with it.
As if it some impartment did desire
To you alone.
Look, with what courteous action
It waves you to a more removèd ground.
But do not go with it.

BURTON.

It will not speak; then I will follow it.

GIELGUD. Stop – let's stop it there.

Beat.

BURTON. I will do that a thousand times better.

He paces. Annoyed with himself.

GIELGUD. No. No. That was interesting. A solid third try. No polish required. The adage stands from our previous: Don't set your readings. You've got to listen and refresh your ear each time.

I must say, I like this pacing you're doing now, Richard. It's nice. Keeps the feeling of the cold. You've got to walk about to keep your circulation going.

BURTON. Good. That's good.

GIELGUD. When I last did *Lear* – the actor playing Gloucester – his only concession to the storm was to fasten his top button.

There's laughter.

MILLI. I've lost my pencil.

GIELGUD. Jessica, if you may –

JESSICA looks quickly for a pencil, REDFIELD notices.

REDFIELD. I have one.

He hurries over and hands a pencil to MILLI.

GIELGUD. I think it might be interesting for our Ghost to be played as a shadow. Let's make the decision that he's – umm – halfway up the wall, above this chair here – mark it with your eyes. We'll choose similar in the theatre.

MILLI. And this shadow… has your voice?

GIELGUD. If the company will have me.

The company reacts positively.

LINDA. What will the Ghost look like?

GIELGUD. Don't let's get overconcerned with the technical. It truly doesn't matter what the Ghost looks like if the audience believes that you – Richard – are seeing the face of your dead father. That is what we need. Just. That.

There's a beat. BURTON nods. But he doesn't like what he's smelling.

BURTON. I only hope 'that' can be found.

GIELGUD *realises he may have overstepped.*

GIELGUD. The speech is delightfully designed – 'Angels and ministers of grace defend us!' He needs every hallowed thing he can gather. And then – he sees it and now we see the devotion 'Hamlet, King, father.' He will follow that Ghost anywhere.

BURTON. Well, I'll do my best to capture that devotion.

GIELGUD *is not sure of the temperature of the room.*

GIELGUD. Dear boy, these are just words to take you along the path. Please, take from my direction what you choose.

We sit in the discomfort for a moment and then MILLI *tries to be helpful.*

MILLI. Should I – scream? When the Ghost appears?

GIELGUD. We can play with that. Feels a bold decision. It's a wire walk, we will walk together.

BURTON. Do I want him to come?

GIELGUD. Your father?

BURTON. Yes.

GIELGUD. What an interesting question. Let's keep going and see what we learn: 'Do not, my Lord.'

Scene Four

Day Eight – 'A Dream Itself is But a Shadow'

GIELGUD *is sat eating sandwiches.*

REDFIELD. Sir John, have you a moment?

GIELGUD. For you, dear boy, I have at least two – moments. Possibly three. But only if you're charming. Which you are. So three.

REDFIELD. You're eating –

GIELGUD. Merely a sandwich.

REDFIELD. You get so little time to yourself, I'm sorry to interrupt your sandwich…

GIELGUD. It is a poor sandwich, you interrupt nothing. How would you like to use your first moment?

REDFIELD *smiles, he doesn't quite understand the stakes here, but he knows* GIELGUD *is playing with him.*

REDFIELD. By asking – how are you – are you enjoying things?

GIELGUD. Ah, how sweet, that you care about my well-being. A waste of a moment, but all the same. I think it's all going splendidly, don't you?

REDFIELD *hesitates.*

Ah, you don't.

GIELGUD *dumps the sandwich in a waste bin.*

Alas, poor sandwich, I knew him, Horatio. Are you here to note the director?

REDFIELD. I just don't know what I'm playing…

GIELGUD. The great surprise of it is none of us do. You'd make a good Horatio, have you ever played him?

REDFIELD. No.

GIELGUD. It's an irritating role. Sort of tops and tails things without ever really challenging the meat. If I were noting him, Uncle Will, I'd tell him to merge Horatio, Rosencrantz and Guildenstern into one. It's too many people for an audience to cope with. You're a splendid Guildenstern, by the way. Very surprising. Funny. I'm enjoying it.

REDFIELD. Thank you. But –

GIELGUD. Curious, isn't it? How Shakespeare always uses three young men –

REDFIELD. Mercutio, Balthasar and Benvolio.

GIELGUD. Lorenzo, Bassanio and Gratiano. But each must be a separate individual and personality and to be fair to Uncle Will – mostly they are –

REDFIELD. I don't know where I come from, what I mean to Hamlet...

GIELGUD. Are you simply a cue line for what's ahead?

REDFIELD. Sometimes it seems as if I am.

GIELGUD. It's his play. Annoying because it's such a good part. But everyone else is simply serving his emotional journey. It's necessary for him to steal it utterly. Were I you...

REDFIELD. You wouldn't have taken my role.

GIELGUD. Nonsense, I played Gaev in *The Cherry Orchard* only recently.

REDFIELD. A better part than Guildenstern.

GIELGUD. And I played Rosencrantz at the Royal Court in – let's see – 1926.

REDFIELD. When you were... twenty-two maybe? I am not twenty-two. I am here for you. I wanted to be directed by you.

GIELGUD. Good. I'm here for you. I want to direct you.

REDFIELD. You are not understanding me...

GIELGUD. I am. You had other starrier parts on offer with better paycheques. You're here because you think I will make you a better actor. In future roles. You're here to be educated by Sir John Gielgud.

REDFIELD. Yes.

GIELGUD. And yet I cannot make you a better actor.

Beat. The words sit hard.

REDFIELD. If you were to play Guildenstern, what would you do?

GIELGUD. Firstly, I would not concern myself with making sense. Words should make sense. But not feelings. And secondly, I'd give a different note each time I entered. I'd play a different instrument. I'd determinedly try to dazzle people into believing I'm more significant than I am.

REDFIELD. Thank you.

GIELGUD. I fear I've disappointed you.

REDFIELD. Burton will need it too. Direction. Help.

GIELGUD *makes a decision and exits the room.*

GIELGUD. I detect a bitterness in your voice. We will find our way together, dear boy. You will see.

Scene Five

Day Nine – 'Caviar to the General'

BURTON *is trying out a sword. Twirling it around in all directions.*

BURTON. Something heavier maybe?

JESSICA. We can find something heavier.

BURTON. Can you fight – ?

JESSICA. Only on Wednesdays…

She smiles at him and twirls the sword as she carries it offstage.

GIELGUD. Shall we get back to it?

BURTON. Your assistant is flirting with me.

GIELGUD. Hamlet hasn't seen them for years, so it takes him a moment to recognise them. He is very surprised to see them and is friendly toward them until the point that he catches them conferring behind his back.

FOWLER. But we're just pleased to see him, is that right?

GIELGUD. Yes. Yes. Probably. What did you do last time?

FOWLER. We were pleased.

GIELGUD. Then do that – then try not being pleased this time.

He consults his notes.

Jessica, I can't read this…

JESSICA. Many confines, wards and dungeons…

GIELGUD. Ah yes, I think the reading should be '*Many* confines, wards and dungeons,' Richard.

BURTON.
Many confines, wards and dungeons.

GIELGUD. No. No. Richard, '<u>*Many*</u> confines, wards and dungeons.'

BURTON (*half in jest*). Don't you *dare* give me a line-reading.

GIELGUD. Do remember, you mustn't be too sharp with Rosencrantz and Guildenstern in their first scene or else the recorder scene will be anticipated. When Hamlet says 'What a piece of work is a man', they are the men he is referring to, and he plays it to them as an expression of what he wants them to represent. Otherwise, they just stand there with nothing to do and look like supers.

REDFIELD. A shame for all concerned.

BURTON *laughs*.

GIELGUD. Then Hamlet gets angry when they laugh at the end on 'Man delights not me'. Rosencrantz quickly changes the subject and thinks of The Players. He gets this idea suddenly. Then the whole tone of the scene changes. Everyone is relieved and happy. The Players are coming.

BURTON. This feels like the first positive thought he has – The
Players, that's something I can use.

GIELGUD. Yes. Yes. Lovely. Lean in to the excitement. Shall
we play?

'My honoured Lord'…

REDFIELD.
My honoured Lord!

FOWLER.
My most dear Lord!

BURTON.
My excellent good friends! How dost thou, Guildenstern?
Ah, Rosencrantz! Good lads, how do you both?

FOWLER.
As the indifferent children of the earth.

REDFIELD.
Happy, in that we are not over-happy.
On Fortune's cap we are not the very button.

BURTON.
What news?

FOWLER.
None, my Lord, but that the world's grown honest.

BURTON.
Then is doomsday near: but your news is not true. Let me
question more in particular. What have you, my good
friends, deserved at the hands of Fortune, that she sends you
to prison hither?

REDFIELD.
Prison, my Lord?

BURTON.
Denmark's a prison.

FOWLER.
Then is the world one.

BURTON.

A goodly one; in which there are many confines, wards and dungeons, Denmark being one o'th'worst.

FOWLER.

We think not so, my Lord.

BURTON.

Why, then 'tis none to you. For there is nothing either good or bad but thinking makes it so. To me it is a prison.

FOWLER.

Why, then your ambition makes it one. 'Tis too narrow for your mind.

BURTON.

O God, I could be bounded in a nutshell and count myself a King of infinite space, were it not that I have bad dreams. What make you at Elsinore?

FOWLER.

To visit you, my Lord, no other occasion.

BURTON.

Beggar that I am, I am even poor in thanks; but I thank you: and sure, dear friends, my thanks are too dear a halfpenny. Were you not sent for? Is it a free visitation?

GIELGUD.

'Is it your own inclining?'

BURTON.

Is it your own inclining? Is it a free visitation? Come, come, deal justly with me: come, come; nay, speak.

REDFIELD.

What should we say, my Lord?

BURTON.

Why, any thing, but to th'purpose. You were sent for, and there is a kind of confession in your looks which your modesties have not craft enough to colour: I know the good King and Queen have sent for you.

FOWLER.

To what end, my Lord?

BURTON.
That you must teach me. But let me conjure you, by the obligation of our ever-preserved love, be even and direct with me, whether you were sent for, or no?

FOWLER (*aside to* REDFIELD).
What say you?

BURTON (*aside*).
Nay, then, I have an eye of you – If you love me, hold not off.

REDFIELD.
My lord, we were sent for.

BURTON.
I will tell you why. So shall my anticipation prevent your discovery, and your secrecy to the King and Queen moult no feather. I have of late – but wherefore I know not – lost all my mirth, forgone all custom of exercises, and indeed it goes so heavily with my disposition that this goodly frame, the earth, seems to me a sterile promontory, this most excellent canopy, the air – look you, this brave o'erhanging firmament, this majestical roof fretted with golden fire – why, it appeareth nothing to me but a foul and pestilent congregation of vapours. What a piece of work is a man! How noble in reason! How infinite in faculties, in form and moving how express and admirable! In action how like an angel! In apprehension how like a god! The beauty of the world! The paragon of animals! And yet, to me, what is this quintessence of dust? Man delights not me. Nor woman neither, though by your smiling you seem to say so.

FOWLER.
My Lord, there was no such stuff in my thoughts.

BURTON.
Why did ye laugh then, when I said 'Man delights not me'?

GIELGUD. Play the desperation, Rosencrantz.

FOWLER.
To think, my Lord, if you delight not in man, what Lenten entertainment The Players shall receive from you. We coted them on the way, and hither are they coming to offer you service.

GIELGUD. Play half the desperation, Rosencrantz –

FOWLER (*unsure*). Again?

GIELGUD. Flatter me –

FOWLER.
To think, my Lord, if you delight not in man, what Lenten entertainment The Players shall receive from you. We coted them on the way, and hither are they coming to offer you service.

GIELGUD. Now find the excitement and fraternity –

FOWLER.
To think, my lord, if you delight not in man, what Lenten entertainment The Players shall receive from you. We coted them on the way, and hither are they coming to offer you service.

GIELGUD (*with good caution*). How wonderful. I liked them all. Very good. Very good. I liked your sly smile then, Dick. Very precise. And your 'piece of work is a man' – very powerful. As one would expect.

Beat.

BURTON. Not further? I was ready to give you my hawk and handsaw?

GIELGUD. Next time I'll let you run on.

BURTON. I felt a little – off –

REDFIELD. Me too.

BURTON. The connection wasn't quite made.

GIELGUD. It felt very strong from this angle.

BURTON. I'm not still enough yet. Stillness is most important. I know that.

Beat. GIELGUD *is trying to work out how to address his thoughts.*

GIELGUD. Perhaps one small thing, have a care as to how much blood you let us smell at this stage. Hamlet is desperate but not yet broken – he is still reaching for ideas –

BURTON. 'Man delights not me, nor woman neither'. He's lost his desire for life…

GIELGUD. Indeed he has, but you must gradually let us in to the abattoir – do not fling open the door and have us dance in the entrails just yet.

BURTON *frowns and moves away.*

No, don't scowl – it is all to come, we must just make sure all the passengers are in the carriage before driving it off the cliff…

BURTON. Granville-Barker?

GIELGUD. Sorry?

BURTON. '…all the passengers are in the carriage before driving it off the cliff.' Is that Granville-Barker?

GIELGUD. No, it is pure Gielgud.

Beat. He laughs. The others don't.

Final thing. Let's get away from Rosencrantz and Guildenstern as a double act. Let's make Rosencrantz attempt to be terribly subtle and intelligent like Claudius, and Guildenstern can be more like the Queen – not too bright, lazy, yet kindly.

BURTON. That's a big note to lump them with –

GIELGUD. Thankfully they're big actors.

REDFIELD. It does – contradict – what you said before about the need for concert between them –

BURTON. Contradiction is the Sir John way. Apparently you take from his direction what you choose.

GIELGUD (*aware of danger*). Quite so.

BURTON. Like grapes, when some are juicy and others are bad.

A match flares between them.

GIELGUD. Let's try it again, play a little more. It's a splendid scene. You're doing it marvellously. Let's try again.

The actors resume position.

REDFIELD.
My honoured Lord!

Scene Six

Day Ten – 'Give Me That Man That is Not Passion's Slave'

BURTON *is alone in his hotel room. He has a glass of Scotch in his hands. He has shopping bags at his feet, from Barneys and Saks, etc.*

TAYLOR *appears in the doorway. In a dressing gown.*

TAYLOR. Another drink is it?

BURTON. Like you haven't been at it all day.

TAYLOR. I've had a few.

BURTON. You're absolutely sloshed and soon I will be too.

TAYLOR. I'm bored, what's your excuse?

BURTON. I'm bored too.

TAYLOR. You're in rehearsal, I'm stuck here.

BURTON. You want me to invite someone over to play with again?

TAYLOR. No. No. I'm increasingly bored of you in company, you make me feel like an egg. You're so – crass and – unnecessary.

BURTON *pulls out an item of clothing from one of his bags. He looks at it and then discards it. He rummages until he finds the clothes he wants.*

He begins to get changed. Pulling off his top, and struggling with his trousers.

What are you doing?

BURTON. Can you make me another?

TAYLOR. No.

BURTON. I'd like a Beefeater. Like that young actor who couldn't stop ogling you –

TAYLOR. No.

BURTON. Then a simple Scotch for this simple sod. Has that – new order been brought up?

BURTON *stumbles over his trousers and lands flat on the floor.*

There's a silence.

Ow.

TAYLOR *starts to laugh.*

TAYLOR. You ridiculous man.

BURTON. Don't laugh.

TAYLOR. I will.

BURTON. I could have broken my neck.

TAYLOR. That would have been even funnier. 'Richard Burton broke his neck today changing his trousers.' They'd all think I was operating some sort of sex dungeon.

He rises.

BURTON.
Let none presume
To wear an undeservèd dignity.

TAYLOR. Is that *Hamlet*?

BURTON. *Merchant of Venice*.

TAYLOR. You're learning lines to the wrong play, dear.

BURTON. Should we fuck?

TAYLOR. With you in that state? No.

BURTON. You're the one in a dressing gown.

TAYLOR. I rather thought it was – I don't know what I thought…

BURTON *begins putting on his clothes.*

BURTON. I'm not that sloshed.

TAYLOR. No. You're angry. I never like fucking you when you're angry.

BURTON. Shame.

TAYLOR. *The Merchant of Venice*. There's a part in that for me, isn't there?

BURTON. No.

TAYLOR. Why not?

BURTON. You're too sexy for Portia.

TAYLOR. What a skill it is to know your wife's limits so well...

BURTON. You're offended by that?

TAYLOR. 'Physician, heal thyself.'

BURTON. What does that mean?

TAYLOR. And that's not Shakespeare, honey, that's – well, Jesus, I believe. Luke 4:23. 'Ye will surely say unto me this proverb, "Physician, heal thyself": whatsoever we have heard done in Capernaum, do also here in thy country.' Christian Science wasn't altogether lost on me.

When dressed, BURTON *stands and looks at himself in the mirror.*

BURTON. What do you think?

TAYLOR. That the man admires himself too much.

BURTON. This is my costume I think. I picked it up today.

TAYLOR. That's what you intend to wear onstage?

BURTON. Yes.

TAYLOR. For your supposed 'rehearsal clothes' when you're presenting this 'rehearsed production'.

BURTON. Yes. Does it work?

TAYLOR. You look like a Prince.

BURTON. Thank you.

TAYLOR. But isn't what Sir John is trying to do – rehearsal clothes –

BURTON. These are rehearsal clothes.

TAYLOR. Are they now?

BURTON. You think I should wear something less –

TAYLOR. Black, sleek and sinewy. Yes.

BURTON. But I like these.

TAYLOR. Then you'll wear those whatever I say.

BURTON. They suit me.

TAYLOR. You look wonderful, but not like you're going to rehearsal.

BURTON. I'm beginning to get bored of the whole concept.

TAYLOR. It was your concept.

BURTON. He claims not, he claims now it's his. And now he's summoning me for a 'private rehearsal'? Fuck it, I'm getting another drink.

He exits.

TAYLOR *is left.*

She stands a moment.

And then she starts to dance. Just a little jaunty dance around the room.

She hears him approach, she stops dancing.

I always liked the idea of you in a church. A little cherubic choirgirl.

TAYLOR. My bone structure was always a little too pronounced to convince as a cherub.

He drinks from his glass.

BURTON. You look beautiful tonight. Have I already told you that?

TAYLOR. I'm in a dressing gown.

BURTON. Certain women have the shape for gowns. Others are subsumed by them. Look like washerwomen. But you – fit it like a –

TAYLOR. Smelly old whore.

BURTON. I have upset you –

TAYLOR.
A smelly old whore
Who was once a cherub
But now is no more.

BURTON. You can play Portia if you want to.

TAYLOR. How kind of you to think so.

BURTON. We'll perform it in Italian perhaps –

TAYLOR. I wouldn't have thought that wise.

BURTON. Zeffirelli will direct us. We'll do it at the Colosseum. No we'll build our own theatre. Host it in the open air in a giant vineyard. Have toga'd waiters bring giant quaffs of wine to the patrons as they sit.

TAYLOR. Sounds positively wanton. May we drink too?

BURTON. We'll drink, dance and be merry. And no one will notice you're horribly miscast.

TAYLOR *looks at him, enjoying the danger he is playing with.*

TAYLOR. I should have played Juliet before I got too old.

BURTON. You'd be the first Juliet for whom Capulet's words would ring entirely true, 'you green-sickness carrion' – 'you tallow-face'.

He laughs to himself. She doesn't join him. He doesn't mind.

Perhaps I should try going to rehearsals drunk.

TAYLOR. That doesn't sound smart –

BURTON. He's so revolting, maybe he'd be better sloshed.

TAYLOR. You're being a card.

BURTON.
'How all occasions do inform against me,
And spur my dull revenge.'

TAYLOR. Give me more.

BURTON. I will not.

TAYLOR.
  'How all occasions do inform against me,
  And spur my dull revenge.'

BURTON. It's the frantic self-pity of it. He's disgusting.

TAYLOR. I'm sure you can redeem him.

BURTON. He's irredeemable.

TAYLOR. Let me come to rehearsals. Let me see you do it.

BURTON. No.

TAYLOR. Why not?

BURTON. Because you're too excited to go. It'd be
  embarrassing.

TAYLOR. Other wives and husbands can come surely.

BURTON. No other wives and husbands can come. He'd
  probably let you come because you're Elizabeth Taylor but
  then Elizabeth Taylor would be watching and it'd spoil every
  single performance occurring onstage.

TAYLOR. I think it's because you fancy your Ophelia.

BURTON. Oh no. She's awful.

TAYLOR. What was the name? That costume bag who you
  constantly flirted around to get me jealous –

BURTON. I did no such thing.

TAYLOR. And then you told me – quite openly – the way to
  attract a woman is to pay a lot of attention to other women.
  And I was thoroughly confused.

BURTON. Were you?

TAYLOR. Kissing all the girls to make me cry? What crude and
  ridiculous behaviour in one so desperate to be sophisticated.

BURTON. We shouldn't do *Merchant*. We should do *Taming of
  the Shrew*, at The Old Vic. Have Tony Richardson direct us.
  He understands poisonous women.

TAYLOR. It was me who seduced you, if you didn't know. The
  costume lady did nothing for me. You did everything.

BURTON. And why on earth would you have wanted me?

TAYLOR. Because you're gruff, and perplexing, and you look good in slacks, honey.

He smiles at her.

But this – your doubt – is boring…

He looks at her, unsure whether she means it.

And boring your wife when she's already bored? That's unforgivable.

BURTON. You're the one who thinks we will be laughed at.

TAYLOR. I'm sorry?

BURTON. 'Physician, heal thyself.' You were referring to my Hamlet. You are saying I am miscast.

TAYLOR. Ahhh that's what this is. Let the record read it was RB who bought his inadequacy into the conversation, not ET. Of course you can play Hamlet. You can play anything. You're the finest actor I ever went to bed with.

BURTON. I can feel the dirty pencils sharpening. 'Burton desperately overreaches as the threadbare production collapses around him.'

TAYLOR. Then walk, honey. We walk now. They'll be angry, sure. They'll sue. But then we will make a movie or two and all will be paid up and forgotten. We'll go to London and do *Merchant of Venice*. We'll go to Rome and do *Shrew*.

BURTON. I need another drink.

TAYLOR. You really don't.

BURTON. Walk. That is your advice? Run – walk.

TAYLOR. No. You're not listening. You can walk or you can stay. It's your *choice*.

Beat.

The good stuff is never easy, you taught me that.

BURTON. And I believe it.

Beat. BURTON *reflects.*

TAYLOR. So?

Beat.

Do I book a plane?

BURTON. No.

She has her answer.

TAYLOR. You don't need clothes to be a Prince. You are a Prince. And Princes stay and fight. Or the true ones do.

BURTON *softens. He smiles.*

BURTON. I do so enjoy it when you're right.

TAYLOR. Is it really so hard?

BURTON. He doesn't have control of it.

TAYLOR. You mean he doesn't have control of you?

BURTON. I'm his Hamlet. Surely he must have control of me. Perhaps this private rehearsal will – improve matters...

TAYLOR *smiles.*

TAYLOR. Come here. Kiss me.

BURTON. Now I may approach?

TAYLOR. You know I never can resist you when you're vulnerable.

BURTON *grins.*

This is how I'd do it. This is how I'd play Portia.

BURTON. The Bible. Quoting the Bible at me like a –

TAYLOR. Kiss me.

He walks over and kisses her.

They begin to have sex.

Scene Seven

Day Eleven – 'Something is Rotten in the State of Denmark'

GIELGUD *is studying a model box.*

BURTON *enters and* GIELGUD *looks up.*

GIELGUD. Thank you so much for giving me – this – time.
I thought it might be useful to have a moment – just the two
of us – look at a few key pieces…

BURTON. Of course.

GIELGUD. Perhaps iron out a few key ideas…

BURTON. Is that the finalised –

GIELGUD. Yes, Ben's model box, I thought you deserved an
exclusive look…

BURTON *approaches the box and looks inside.*

Side platform, main platform – there are four different exits
from – main stage – side stage – left entrance, right entrance,
and the doors here at the back.

BURTON *studies it all carefully.*

BURTON. We still have the exit up-right?

GIELGUD. Yes.

BURTON. Good.

GIELGUD. Simple. It's simple. Won't win him the Tony, but he
knows that. You will win the Tony of course.

Beat.

Have you won a Tony? I've never won one for my acting.
Won one for my directing curiously. But it's so hard to –
I mean, the whole matter of judging anything… Vulgar.

BURTON. Yes. I feel the same about the Academy. About Oscar.

GIELGUD. It seems to me, Richard, and I found it too in
playing the part, that in the concern with details in each
single scene one forgets the main motivation which must
progress through the part as a whole. You said you felt this
and I've felt it so often too.

BURTON. It's a play about a man who can't make up his mind –

GIELGUD. Larry said the same – about the film –

BURTON. You don't agree?

GIELGUD. It doesn't matter what I think, it's about what you think. If it were me – when I played it – it's about a man who cannot reconcile his own conscience with the world as he sees it, but who is able to come to this reconciliation by the end of the play.

BURTON. He can't fight and then he can.

GIELGUD. For whatever reason – you feel – for whatever reason feels right to you.

BURTON. Good.

Beat.

GIELGUD. Hamlet, in my opinion, begins apathetically and can't rouse himself to any action, even though he hates the King. The Ghost gives him purpose and doubt, Ophelia's death gives him responsibility. These are all elements we must see.

BURTON. These are all elements I can show.

Beat.

GIELGUD. What would you like to try?

BURTON. Rogue and peasant slave?

GIELGUD. Splendid. Your audience awaits – (*He indicates.*) You've asked your friends to leave – and you do not want to be alone, you hate being alone – but you must be alone – 'go away, I must think this out'.

BURTON.
Now I am alone.
O, what a rogue and peasant slave am I!
Is it not monstrous that this player here,
But in a fiction, in a dream of passion,
Could force his soul so to his own conceit
That from her working all his visage wanned,
Tears in his eyes, distraction in his aspect,

A broken voice, and his whole function suiting
With forms to his conceit? And all for nothing!
For Hecuba!

GIELGUD. Richard, if I may, there's a music in this speech that
I think might give us help here.

BURTON. What music?

GIELGUD. This speech is a gentle build. Is it not monstrous?
One phrase poses, the other answers. Until eventually a
climax is found. Hear the Handel in it, it's Zadok – da-ba-ba-
da-ba-ba da-ba-ba-ba-ba...

BURTON. I'm not sure I – without meaning to cause a problem –
I'm not sure I hear the music like that – I hear it differently –

GIELGUD. Exciting. What is your music?

BURTON. I'm not sure the music I hear has been written.

GIELGUD. Even greater still.

BURTON. But I hear the – note –

They both smile.

GIELGUD. From the top again.

BURTON *sways, considering the music.*

BURTON.
Now I am alone.
O, what a rogue and peasant slave am I!
Is it not monstrous that this player here,
But in a fiction, in a dream of passion,
Could force his soul so to his own conceit
That from her working all his visage wanned,
Tears in his eyes, distraction in his aspect,
A broken voice, and his whole function suiting
With forms to his conceit? And all for nothing!
For Hecuba!
What's Hecuba to him, or he to Hecuba
That he should weep for her? What would he do,
Had he the motive and the cue for passion
That I have –

GIELGUD. Good. Good.

Beat. BURTON *holds himself back as* GIELGUD *steps forward.*

Have a care as to shouting. You shout wonderfully, both you and Larry do – two splendid cornets. I am a violin, I'm afraid, not too good at shouting. But these hunting calls you do so well can be tiresome when sounded too often. Don't overuse it.

Beat. BURTON *gives him nothing.*

It's a wonderful weapon, but it's your last weapon. Use it only when all else fails. 'He would drown' –

BURTON.
He would drown the stage with tears
And cleave the general ear with horrid speech,
Make mad the guilty and appal the free,
Confound the ignorant, and amaze indeed
The very faculties of eyes and ears.
Yet I,
A dull and muddy-mettled rascal, peak
Like John-a-dreams, unpregnant of my cause,
And can say nothing; no, not for a King,
Upon whose property and most dear life
A damned defeat was made. Am I a coward?

He takes a monstrous pause, he's growing into this now.

Who calls me villain? Breaks my pate across?
Plucks off my beard, and blows it in my face?
Tweaks me by the nose?
Gives me the lie i'th'throat
As deep as to the lungs? Who does me this?
Ha!
'Swounds, I should take it: for it cannot be
But I am pigeon-livered and lack gall
To make oppression bitter, or ere this
I should ha' fatted all the region kites
With this slave's offal. Bloody, bawdy villain!
Remorseless, treacherous, lecherous, kindless villain!

And the heights he hits are too much for GIELGUD.

GIELGUD. Too much. Too much. '*Remorseless, treacherous, lecherous, kindless villain!*'

Beat, there's a silence, BURTON *smoulders.*

I'm sorry, carry on…

BURTON. I know your instincts are to give line-readings at every available opportunity, but perhaps find another way of expressing direction.

GIELGUD. Awful of me. Carry on…

There's a silence.

BURTON.
Remorseless, treacherous, lecherous, kindless villain!
O, vengeance!
Why, what an ass am I! This is most brave,
That I, the son of a dear father murdered,
Prompted to my revenge by heaven and hell,
Must, like a whore, unpack my heart with words,
And fall a-cursing, like a very drab,
A scullion!
Fie upon't! Foh! About, my brains! Hum – I have heard
That guilty creatures sitting at a play
Have, by the very cunning of the scene
Been struck so to the soul that presently
They have proclaimed their malefactions.
For murder, though it have no tongue, will speak
With most miraculous organ.

GIELGUD. Let the thoughts come to you. Let them come.

BURTON. THE THOUGHTS ARE BLOODY COMING TO ME.

There's a silence. GIELGUD *gestures for* BURTON *to carry on. He does so with a glower.*

I'll have these Players
Play something like the murder of my father
Before mine uncle. I'll observe his looks;
I'll tent him to the quick. If he but blench,
I know my course. The spirit that I have seen
May be a devil, and the Devil hath power
T'assume a pleasing shape. Yea, and perhaps

Out of my weakness and my melancholy,
As he is very potent with such spirits,
Abuses me to damn me. I'll have grounds
More relative than this. The play's the thing
Wherein I'll catch the conscience of the King.

BURTON *stands a moment more, processing.*

GIELGUD. Such a commanding advertisement for theatre, don't you think?

BURTON. Yes.

GIELGUD. Theatre as a trap. An empathy hole into which huge bears can fall. I always found it very moving. The idea of this. I'm not sure I'd do it as he does. But I admire the sentiment of it.

BURTON *says nothing.*

Why make theatre? What's in it for you? You, who have everything?

BURTON. Why act at all?

GIELGUD. You'd rather not?

BURTON. I'm not sure.

GIELGUD. You who is offered everything looks down upon it and says 'perhaps I don't like these offerings'.

BURTON. Is that your problem with me – arrogance?

GIELGUD. I have no problem with you. I am a great admirer of you.

BURTON. And I of you. I have always enjoyed acting with you.

GIELGUD. Dear boy, I'm aware of the sizeable crumbs you give me from your plate, without you I wouldn't have got *Becket*, which I thoroughly enjoyed.

BURTON. So why hasn't this worked?

There's a silence. This question penetrates.

GIELGUD. The Welshman's worrisome bluntness sails up the River Severn. I wouldn't say it hasn't worked – I'd say that we have yet to find the right ship.

BURTON. The current is strong, Sir John, we're two weeks in, we will sink if we don't find our rudder.

GIELGUD *nods, this is hard on him.*

GIELGUD. So let's think of the problem that's upon us. The actor is stuck with the character, but the character is also stuck with the actor. We need to find a place where these two meet. I couldn't play the same Hamlet as Larry, and he couldn't play the same Hamlet as I – my point is, you may claim – the point is, you may think I am trying to persuade you to play my Hamlet, but you are wrong –

BURTON. Your Hamlet was superior to Larry's.

GIELGUD. He won the Academy Award for his. Nonsense, like you say. But – all the same –

BURTON. I understand what you're saying, and I'm grateful you're not trying to distort me –

They are still circling each other, but finally GIELGUD *goes for the kill.*

GIELGUD. But I am. Trying to distort you. Because this character must. The trouble we have, dear boy, is that you are instructed in the first scene of the play by the ghost of your father to kill a man, and I don't doubt for a second you'd do it. *Immediately.*

BURTON. I am poorly suited to the role.

GIELGUD. So you must adapt yourself, to make this Hamlet yours. Find the central question.

BURTON. Play it more like you, when that is expressly what you told me, just two moments ago, not to do.

GIELGUD. No, but I hope you might accept that I have some skills which could be useful to yours.

BURTON. Your Hamlet is not mine.

GIELGUD. Of course not.

BURTON. The trouble is your sing-song approach.

GIELGUD. I can't sing, dear boy.

BURTON. It's a little old-fashioned. That mellifluous voice, Shakespeare-with-all-the-trimmings. You do it better than anyone else alive. But that is not what I want to play and I do not believe it's what the audience want to see.

GIELGUD. Audience receipts would undoubtedly show you to be correct. I am yesterday's stale toast. Quite right.

There's a dangerous air.

BURTON. I came to you for this job –

GIELGUD. I repeat – I am grateful for your beneficence.

BURTON. Because I want your discipline, your understanding, but I think you also have something to learn from me –

GIELGUD. So much. May I sit on your knee –

BURTON. About spontaneity. The audience need to feel the play is alive.

GIELGUD*'s frustration is clear.*

GIELGUD. The audience need to feel the story is possible, and it is impossible the way you're playing it.

BURTON. Goddamnit, man – will you not listen to me?

GIELGUD. I HAVE DONE NOTHING BUT – AND I BELIEVE I AM THE DIRECTOR. It is I who should speak.

BURTON. I am going to be up on that stage and you've armed me with nothing, because you are not directing me, you're directing yourself.

GIELGUD. You are going to be up on that stage and give them nothing but your bloated ego.

BURTON *becomes a viper, he's good at damage and he's ready for this.*

BURTON. I didn't know how angry you were –

GIELGUD. Angry –

BURTON. Can't find your place, is it? They've given Larry the South Bank, the Royal Court seems to have set stall in the West End and that Shakespeare lot in Stratford sure as hell

don't want you with their modern ways. Where's the King
Lear that will cause all to lay down before you –

GIELGUD *is viper-quick back.*

GIELGUD. I gave my Lear at twenty-seven. 1931. The Old Vic.
A bit too young yes, but I'd played everyone else by then
and I needed the challenge.

BURTON. So great. So young. And now – ignored. Poor old
homeless Sir John.

GIELGUD. I've got old doing what I love, dear, you're not so
young yourself, and unlike me you've wasted your time
getting rich, fat and famous rather than developing your
craft. If you're not in love with acting you should be,
because it is the finest job, and because it deserves your love.
I saw your last Hamlet, it was ridiculous. But you are a good
actor. You have the soul and the wit of a good actor. Listen to
me. You will only prove yourself if you listen.

BURTON. Fuck you.

BURTON *leaves the rehearsals.*

Scene Eight

Day Twelve – 'A Great Man's Memory'

GIELGUD *is sitting in the rehearsal room hunched over
a microphone leading to a three-track recorder.*

GIELGUD.
    I am thy father's spirit
    Doomed for a certain term to walk the night,
    And for the day confined to fast in fires,
    Till the foul crimes done in my days of nature
    Are burnt and purged away –

There is a knock. He clicks off the tape.

Enter.

JESSICA *enters*.

JESSICA. I interrupted a recording.

GIELGUD. Ah, dear girl – don't look so scared. I asked for you, didn't I?

And I am not recording. Merely placing them down for time.

JESSICA. Yes.

GIELGUD. I'm struggling with Ophelia.

JESSICA. The character or the actor?

GIELGUD. The character is an awful part. No, I mean the actor...

JESSICA. She's struggling too I think.

GIELGUD. Do the company like her?

JESSICA. Uh. Yes. I think so.

GIELGUD. Would it be deemed a blood sacrifice from a stumbling director?

JESSICA. You're not stumbling.

There's a pause.

GIELGUD. So should I cut her? Find someone new?

JESSICA. I could arrange some auditions.

GIELGUD. A splendid idea. Let's look and while we look, let's judge.

JESSICA. Yes.

GIELGUD. What do you aspire to?

JESSICA. I'm sorry?

GIELGUD. Direction?

JESSICA. Yes.

GIELGUD *nods*.

GIELGUD. How would you like to direct *Hamlet*?

JESSICA. It wouldn't suit me.

GIELGUD. Fascinating. And here was I ready to offer you the job. Why not?

JESSICA. One, he's a dude, you know…

GIELGUD. Yes, a 'dude', yes.

JESSICA. Two, I don't like him for how he treats Ophelia.

GIELGUD. I didn't know liking him was a prerequisite for wanting to explore him…

JESSICA. Three, because I think there are modern plays I'd – prefer to do.

GIELGUD. A Royal Court-ist. How fascinating. You have an idea for *Look Back in Anger*?

JESSICA. No, I think that's a problem too. But I'd love to direct *The Knack*. Ann Jellicoe.

GIELGUD. I did not see that. I believe Tynan gave it a good notice. He does not like me.

Beat.

The Knack. What it's about?

JESSICA. It's about three men trying to seduce the same woman. But it's also about her and what she wants and… it's mostly about sex…

GIELGUD. Ah sex. Yes. I remember that.

He smiles.

I wish I had seen it.

JESSICA. It's a world I know. I understand.

GIELGUD. And that's what you wish to see? A world you know rather than a Danish court?

JESSICA. I feel like I understand the questions in it better.

Beat.

GIELGUD. She's Welsh too, I think. Miss Jellicoe.

JESSICA. Yes.

Beat.

Is he treating you badly?

GIELGUD. No.

JESSICA. I don't like the way he talks to you.

GIELGUD. Question: Do you like the way I talk to him?

JESSICA. I'm sorry?

GIELGUD. My direction. Do you like that?

JESSICA looks at him.

JESSICA. I think they aren't built like you are.

GIELGUD. No one seems to be any more.

JESSICA. They want more direction than you would want yourself.

GIELGUD. And yet when I give it, they reject it.

JESSICA. Only him. The others are hungry.

GIELGUD. The tragedy of the dolphin feeder, the others feed gladly, but he looks only to the one who doesn't.

JESSICA looks at him a moment more.

Besides, you're wrong, I'm a terrible director for them too. The skin of it feels – distorted somehow.

Beat. He reaches over to the recorder.

I'll try to be better. I'll look up Miss Jellicoe.

JESSICA. I'm being dismissed?

GIELGUD. How sweet of you to notice.

She nods, and makes to stand. She hesitates. And then –

She exits.

He's left. He thinks.

Scene Nine

Day Thirteen – 'Where it Draws Blood'

The stage is quickly filled with actors.

CRONYN. The trouble is you're all learning your lines too fast.

REDFIELD. Sir John asked –

CRONYN. And you seem to be trying to give a finished performance.

REDFIELD. You think I'm making a mistake?

CRONYN. It is too soon for all that. It is not enough to play things ably. A performance must be inevitable.

REDFIELD. Inevitable?

CRONYN. The atmosphere of this rehearsal seems to be, let's all give the best performances we can in the shortest possible time and don't ask any questions…

REDFIELD. I'm questioning.

CRONYN. Are you? Or are you impressing? Our Prince doesn't even know what crown he's wearing and you're fastening your last zipper.

HERLIE. Oh, Hume. Leave the boy alone.

REDFIELD. I'm not a boy.

CRONYN. He's not a boy.

FOWLER. Can I be a boy?

HERLIE. Ask Mr Cronyn about *The Honeys* –

CRONYN. Now now…

HERLIE. Because *those* reviews were inevitable.

CRONYN. Ouch.

REDFIELD. A hard one?

CRONYN. Jessica still has nightmares we're about to go on.

BURTON *walks in. He's a little unsteady. He's drunk.*

MARSH. I liked that play.

CRONYN. You're too young to like that play.

MARSH. I liked something else you were in. What must it have been?

CRONYN. Oh please don't make me list credits. Are you okay, old man?

BURTON. Wonderful, Hume. How are you?

HERLIE. *Big Fish, Little Fish*, you're probably thinking of that.

MARSH. Oh yes, it must be that…

BURTON. About the queers.

GIELGUD *enters – full of fresh determination.*

GIELGUD. Ladies and gentlemen, one of my favourite scenes and frankly, one of my greatest nightmares, welcome to the Player King and Player Queen. George. Christine. You've both been very patient.

VOSKOVEC. We've been very happy watching you all work.

COOPER. We have.

GIELGUD. And I can't wait to see what you have for us. Keep it exciting. All of you. Let it happen before our eyes. Try to forget it's a very famous classic, instead make it an exciting new play which the public – lucky them – has never seen before.

CRONYN. We'll try.

GIELGUD. Wonderful. Thank you. Now, first things first, I'm cutting the dumb show, everyone always thinks it's hilarious in the rehearsal room and it never gets a single laugh onstage…

BURTON. But we're in the rehearsal room?

GIELGUD. Sorry?

BURTON. You're cutting a piece that works in a rehearsal room and we're playing our play in the rehearsal room…

GIELGUD *looks at* BURTON, *unsure.*

GIELGUD. Are you quite well?

BURTON. Happy as a lark.

GIELGUD. How wonderful. Dick, if I may, the way you are playing the role is without procrastination, so this scene now takes on greater purpose.

BURTON. In what way?

GIELGUD. He's questioning the Ghost's reliability. He needs certainty. These honest players are the chance for him to find it.

BURTON. Yes. I see it the same.

GIELGUD. He is filled with excitement and possibility. Can he trap the truth?

BURTON. He wants to.

GIELGUD. So give yourself that stage.

BURTON. I intend to.

GIELGUD. George, Christine, do you have any questions?

VOSKOVEC. We're ready.

GIELGUD. I'd like to run it through to Claudius, Gertrude, Polonius, the whole bunch of you –

HERLIE. The majority of us are entirely ready, Sir John.

She looks dryly at BURTON, *who has read it.*

DRAKE. Standing by.

BURTON. Friends – (*He indicates* REDFIELD.) Romans – (*He indicates* CRONYN.) Cunts – (*He indicates* HERLIE.) we're all ready –

HERLIE. I'm a cunt, am I, darling? How sobering.

CRONYN. Not to worry, love, apparently I'm a Roman. I'm actually from Ontario.

GIELGUD *is fast realising how badly this is going to go.*

GIELGUD. Shall we reschedule? Do this another time?

BURTON. And disappoint Christine and George? Not on your nelly. I want to see this *Hamlet*-that-has-never-been-seen-before.

COOPER. We're happy to wait longer.

VOSKOVEC. We'll fit however you like.

BURTON. How polite you all are, but I insist we press on.

Beat.

GIELGUD. From 'Speak the speech' then...

BURTON.
Speak the speech, I pray you, as I pronounced it to you, trippingly on the tongue: but if you mouth it, as many of our players do, I had as lief the town-crier spoke my lines. Nor do not – ahhh, wonderful.

A WAITER *has come in with a tray of Scotch and sodas.*

GIELGUD. Not now please...

BURTON. No, no, these are from me, I ordered them for the group.

GIELGUD. Scotch and sodas?

BURTON. Yes.

GIELGUD. For everyone?

BURTON. For all that wants them. George, might you partake as a token for your entrance...

GIELGUD *nods.*

GIELGUD. Go ahead.

VOSKOVEC. I'm fine.

COOPER. I'm fine.

BURTON. Surely, Eileen – your reputation would suggest...

HERLIE. I'm fine.

BURTON. Linda, you want to be drunk under that blanket?

MARSH. I'm happy as I am.

BURTON. Lucky you. Rosencrantz?

FOWLER. No.

BURTON. Where's Guildenstern?

REDFIELD. It's William, and no.

BURTON looks around.

BURTON. Come on then, brave knight, you and I must joust alone.

GIELGUD. You expect me to drink one?

BURTON. Of course.

GIELGUD. I am so sorry to inform you of this, but I am afraid I am a professional.

BURTON dead-eyes GIELGUD.

BURTON. It's a lot for me alone. I'll start again, glass in hand, perhaps that's the way to do it in our rehearsal show –

He downs a glass, and then adds soda to another. He picks it up and walks back into character.

Mother, you're frowning at me.

HERLIE. It's a rehearsal, not a brawl, one would expect better behaviour.

BURTON. You're completely right. Hold my glass, Guildenstern.

He hands it to REDFIELD.

Speak the speech, I pray you, as I pronounced it to you – I've lost my place.

Beat.

I am rehearsing. Where are my notes? Surely you have a note – note-giver.

GIELGUD. I fear I've said enough.

BURTON. Do you prefer the term director or note-giver? Or simply Ghost? Perhaps – that might be fun – we could just credit you as 'Ghost' and then 'Ghost director', what say you?

CRONYN. Sir John Gielgud is our director.

BURTON. Guildenstern, my Scotch.

HERLIE. Don't give it him.

REDFIELD. I wasn't intending to.

BURTON.
Speak the speech I pray you – I NEED A NOTE –

Beat. GIELGUD *has a choice.*

GIELGUD. Perhaps give the *I* emphasis… It might unlock the meaning…

BURTON. John, dear, you are in love with pronouns, but *I* am not.

GIELGUD. Ahh – you simply wanted a note in order to disagree with it? That does not surprise me.

BURTON. Let me do it as you, that might help me actually, unlock something –

He does a bad impression. An almost homophobic impression in fact…

Speak the speech, I pray you, as I pronounced it to you, trippingly on the tongue:

CRONYN. Richard…

BURTON.
– but if you mouth it, as many of our players do, I had as lief the town-crier spoke my lines. Nor do not saw the air too much with your hand, thus, but use all gently;

CRONYN. Richard, stop this…

BURTON.
– for in the very torrent, tempest, and, as I may say, whirlwind of your passion, you must acquire and beget a temperance that may give it smoothness. WHY AREN'T I CRYING YET? TEARS, COME FALL FROM MY EYES…

He is laughing quite uproariously.

GIELGUD. You laugh at me.

BURTON. No.

GIELGUD. You laugh at my performance.

BURTON *is still laughing.*

BURTON. How many tears are too many, I suppose is the question I'm asking.

GIELGUD. And you ask that question with laughter?

BURTON. No need to get sensitive, John. Sorry, Sir John. Did I get the emphasis right? *Sir* John. SIR John.

GIELGUD. It's the strangest thing, today I turned up and I was ready to start anew and you turn up drunk?

BURTON (*laughing*).
Speak the speech, I pray you, as I pronounced it to you, with the emphasis on the 'I'. I pray you. I PRAY YOU.

CRONYN. No one else is laughing, Sir John.

There's a silence.

GIELGUD. And yet, kind words, such kindness, thank you, and yet – the shame is that I would rather this particular humiliation didn't have an audience.

HERLIE. You're not being humiliated. He's simply drunk.

BURTON. How dare you?

GIELGUD. Would you mind all leaving?

BURTON. He is dismissing us all. As naughty schoolboys for – laughter. Theatre is supposed to be fun – you asked why I did it and the truth is I do it for fun...

GIELGUD. All of you. Rehearsal's over. Please.

CRONYN. John, don't you think –

GIELGUD. No, I do not. I don't think. I'm sorry. We will all do better tomorrow. Out. Please.

HERLIE. I would like to stay.

GIELGUD. And give pity? No thank you. Jessica, can you make them all leave?

JESSICA. Please.

BURTON. Take a glass of Scotch with you. We'll all congregate in the hall.

HERLIE *slaps* BURTON *hard around the face*.

Out damned spot…

They leave.

BURTON *is almost the last to go. He stands swaying a moment.*

CRONYN. Come on, Dick. Don't make this worse.

He pulls him out of the room.

GIELGUD *is left. There's silence.* JESSICA *re-enters.*

JESSICA. You want me to leave too?

GIELGUD. Oh yes.

Beat.

JESSICA. Sir John, what he said –

GIELGUD. Please say no more, your kind words have truth to them, the trouble is his unkind ones had truth to them too.

JESSICA. There's no truth –

GIELGUD. I knew his Hamlet would not be one that interested me – tremendous actor – but not a Hamlet you see…

Beat.

JESSICA. So why did you – ?

GIELGUD. Because it was the best offer I'd had in quite some time. Can you go please?

She exits.

GIELGUD *sits heavily for a long time. We just watch his pain.*

And then he stands.

He picks up a piece of discarded cloth. He carefully wraps it over himself.

He stands straight, and suddenly he's the Prince of Denmark.

Speak the speech, I pray you, as I pronounced it to you, trippingly on the tongue. But if you mouth it, as many of our players do, I had as lief the town-crier spoke my lines. Nor do not saw the air too much with your hand, thus, but use all gently, for in the very torrent, tempest, and, as I may say, whirlwind of your passion, you must acquire and beget a temperance that may give it smoothness. O, it offends me to the soul to hear a robustious periwig-pated fellow tear a passion to tatters, to very rags, to split the ears of the groundlings, who for the most part are capable of nothing but inexplicable dumbshows and noise: I would have such a fellow whipped for o'erdoing Termagant. It out-Herods Herod: pray you, avoid it.

He holds us, a moment and then a moment more, utterly majestic.

Be not too tame neither, but let your own discretion be your tutor. Suit the action to the word, the word to the action; with this special observance that you o'erstep not the modesty of nature. For anything so o'erdone is from the purpose of playing, whose end, both at the first and now, was and is, to hold, as 'twere, the mirror up to nature. To show virtue her own feature, scorn her own image, and the very age and body of the time his form and pressure. Now this overdone, or come tardy off, though it make the unskilful laugh, cannot but make the judicious grieve. O, there be players that I have seen play, and heard others praise, and that highly, not to speak it profanely, that, neither having th'accent of Christians nor the gait of Christian, pagan, nor man, have so strutted and bellowed that I have thought some of nature's journeymen had made men and not made them well, they imitated humanity so abominably.

He stays standing. His eyes filled with gut-wrenching tears.

Curtain.

Interval.

ACT TWO: THE CUE

Scene One

Day Fifteen – 'The Breathing Time of Day'

TAYLOR *and* GIELGUD *are breakfasting together.*

TAYLOR. They make the most adorable breakfast scones.

GIELGUD. Then I must try them. And everything else you
think I might enjoy. You order for me –

TAYLOR. No.

GIELGUD. Yes.

TAYLOR. I couldn't.

GIELGUD. Why couldn't you?

TAYLOR. Because I'm a vulgarian and you're the best actor
alive.

GIELGUD. You know, the polite thing to say is 'one of the best
actors alive', otherwise you leave out all the other actors
who are also the best actors alive.

TAYLOR. No one holds a candle to you.

GIELGUD. You talk such nonsense.

TAYLOR. Your *Ages of Man* was so good it made me want to
throw up in a bucket.

GIELGUD. I heard you were deranged, I didn't know how
deranged.

TAYLOR. I heard you were wicked. I didn't know how wicked.

GIELGUD. And I heard your eyes were dazzling but I wasn't
prepared how dazzling.

TAYLOR. Anyone can have a set of eyes.

GIELGUD. Your bosom is also tremendous.

TAYLOR *laughs*.

TAYLOR. I *like* you.

GIELGUD. You understand I have – no interest in your bosom?

TAYLOR. I do.

GIELGUD. Other than a professional or scientific curiosity.

TAYLOR. I'll show you mine if you show me yours.

GIELGUD. I fear we'd both be disappointed in our respective responses.

TAYLOR *laughs again. A* WAITER *approaches. He leans in.*

She's ordering for me.

TAYLOR. He'll take the scones. With some smoked salmon…

GIELGUD. Oh no.

TAYLOR. Bacon?

GIELGUD. Yes.

TAYLOR. Two poached eggs?

GIELGUD (*wincing*). Perhaps…

TAYLOR. Scrambled?

GIELGUD (*a frown*). Possibly.

TAYLOR. Fried.

GIELGUD (*a smile*). Undoubtedly.

TAYLOR *laughs*.

TAYLOR. You could have saved some time here, honey, you know that?

GIELGUD. Saving time is vulgar.

TAYLOR. So he'll have bacon and fried eggs and the scones. And hot sauce. To make sure he stays naughty.

WAITER. And for you?

TAYLOR. Egg-white omelette.

GIELGUD. And scones and – why not – smoked salmon.

TAYLOR *thumps the table in delight*.

TAYLOR. Why not indeed?

GIELGUD. And also some hot sauce.

TAYLOR. Sure. And more of this English tea.

WAITER. Of course.

The WAITER *departs with a nod*.

GIELGUD. So – you summoned me.

TAYLOR. I'm here to make a peace accord.

GIELGUD. But he is not here.

TAYLOR. Can you think of anyone worse to broker peace
with? Can you imagine Yalta with Dick Burton? Churchill
would have had a broken jaw and Stalin a bloodied nose,
a lot of Welsh poetry would be spoken and war would still
be raging now.

GIELGUD. I don't really read the newspapers.

TAYLOR. You haven't heard of Yalta?

He's being naughty and they both know it.

GIELGUD. I've a vague – recollection –

TAYLOR. He can't do it. So we can. Peace.

GIELGUD. Are you going to tell me the secret of how to direct
him?

TAYLOR. I've just married the man, I may have some tips.

GIELGUD. You have assets at your disposal I do not.

TAYLOR. And you have assets at your disposal I do not.

GIELGUD *smiles*.

GIELGUD. You're going to give me a speech now about how
much he admires me.

TAYLOR. You know, *he* gives this speech about his father
taking him to see you perform.

GIELGUD. I know. I've heard it. It makes me feel old. He was only twelve years old. And dazzled by me. Just as his father was dazzled.

TAYLOR. It's poppycock. His father didn't give a crap about him or theatre. Pardon my Shakespeare. And no one had any damn money to go to the theatre at that time. And you didn't go anywhere near Port Talbot to perform.

GIELGUD. How close is it to Bristol?

TAYLOR. His father was a drunk. A violent man. He abandoned Dick and Dick was brought up by his sister. A man called Phillip Burton – his teacher and the man whose name Richard took – must have been the one who brought him to see you, by which time Richard would have been at least seventeen. Richard took Phillip's name because he made him feel talented, loved and that he belonged.

GIELGUD. How tragic.

Beat.

No, I do mean that...

TAYLOR. You're a Terry, I'm a – well, I'm a me. You were born in a theatre. Your great-aunt redefined it. Your uncle rebuilt its very stages.

GIELGUD. Gordon's not my uncle, he's my – I'm never quite sure what he was –

TAYLOR. I was born on the silver screen. I was twelve years old when I did *National Velvet. A Princess for me is not such a reach –*

GIELGUD. I saw your Cleopatra it was most –

TAYLOR. *And a Prince for you – seems – natural.* He's a miner's son. A drunk's son. He doesn't understand diffidence because he never saw it. In his world, you either wanted a fight or you didn't.

GIELGUD. Beguiling. Your Cleopatra was beguiling.

TAYLOR. Help him. And he will help you. Fight him and he will fight you.

GIELGUD. I am not a fighter.

Beat.

I am also perhaps not much of a director – but I am trying so hard to be the best one for him...

Beat.

Diffidence – how extraordinary to pick that word –

TAYLOR. It's what *Hamlet*'s about, isn't it? A diffident man making a choice.

GIELGUD. I am trying to help him find it.

TAYLOR. You need to find a new way to do so. I want him to be the definitive Hamlet. Soldier, scholar, Prince... And in your hands...

GIELGUD. He has every chance of being so?

TAYLOR. The classicist who wants to be modern, meeting the modernist who wants to be classical. That's where great fireworks occur.

GIELGUD. I want to be modern, do I?

She grins, she knows how cute she's being.

TAYLOR. Of course you do. Who wouldn't?

GIELGUD. May I ask – did Richard ask you to – intervene this way?

TAYLOR. Of course not. I am here on my own terms. I do most things on my own.

Now, where are our breakfasts? Can't they see we're terribly important and terribly in need of scones.

Scene Two

Day Seventeen – 'To Thine Own Self Be True'

BURTON *is holding court amongst his fellow actors in the rehearsal room.*

BURTON. So – Larry was playing Titus Andronicus – I'm at the opening night – the hand-chopping is approaching – the audience murmurs – Larry, as you know, famous for bold physical effects and has an appetite for letting visible blood – the audience is excited –

GIELGUD *enters at the back of the room.* BURTON *seems to sense he's there.*

If only I knew the speech by heart – but I don't. Titus says a fond and rueful farewell to his hand, and as usual with Shakespeare no sentiment is left unturned. Larry was crooning and moaning and kissing his dear hand for all the world like a lost pathetic child. I tell you, it was thrilling. You know, I've always felt with his acting there's a sense of cogs and wheels going around – well, this time it was gone, this time there was a freshness to it. He brought each finger to his lips, he pressed the palm to his cheek, he turned it this way and that – he murmured to it lovingly – some of the lines were even swallowed, which is not like Larry at all. I was bewitched by the way he moved his mouth about the hand while the other hand caressed it. Such an enchanting design...

BURTON *turns and plays* GIELGUD *into the scene.*

Well, it was a design, for when he reached the end of the speech, he stopped his crooning and caressing, straightened his shoulders, placed his beloved hand against a tabletop, accepted a hatchet from a soldier, swung it a great roundhouse whack through the air as though chopping firewood, let out one of his hair-raising shrieks and bounded across the stage leaving – his own hand, dismembered, we all gasped as one, a few ladies fainted.

He looks around the room.

So why – how – what drew him to give this performance – was it method acting? Sincere feeling? Or just a sense of the psychology of it all? No. He had to do the speech in just that way. He needed all the pauses to give himself time to undo the artificial hand, the bent shoulders and passionate hunch came from having to withdraw his own true hand carefully up his sleeve. The kissing and caressing were to conceal the nuts and bolts and ratchets he was carefully undoing. The whole manner of the speech was merely a smokescreen. A foil for his magic trick. Harry Houdini of The Old Vic.

GIELGUD. Larry is a joy. A great observer of life. Yet at times, I think his observations interfere with the poetry.

BURTON. You may be right.

GIELGUD. Larry imposes such dazzling things on the text. But what of the text itself? Simply the text? What I admire about you, Richard, is you are determined to let the play itself sing.

Beat.

BURTON. I feel I should start by apologising – to the group – and especially you – for treating you so awfully in the last rehearsal. You are one of the true knights of the stage and –

GIELGUD. Shall we leave it there before you genuflect so far your head actually disappears inside my bottom?

There's laughter.

Kind words. Let's rehearse. Polonius. Are you ready to die?

CRONYN. In truth, dear brother, I've been ready for quite some time.

GIELGUD. Now we've struggled with the staging when we looked at this scene previously.

HERLIE. It felt a little exposed.

GIELGUD. But I've had a thought. I am going to bring on a wardrobe rack from here – it will be hung with greatcoats, velvets and furs. Polonius will do his eavesdropping from behind a rack –

BURTON. That could work…

GIELGUD. And you stab him through – let us try some things, Jessica –

BURTON. I'll need a crevice of some kind, so as not to lose the sword by fuzzy velvet – I wish not be seen as weak-fisted.

GIELGUD. Yes, what would look best?

JESSICA *hands him a sword.*

GIELGUD *begins jabbing it through the cloth.*

CRONYN. Just a reminder that an old and distinguished actor is behind that clothing.

BURTON. I'll take care of you.

CRONYN. You are a passionate man. You do not strike me as a fastidious swordsman.

BURTON. I have killed many co-stars.

There's laughter.

JESSICA. None of the swords are sharp.

CRONYN. My dear petal, my heart is so tender it could be penetrated by a cocktail stick.

There's laughter.

GIELGUD *keeps jabbing.*

Now you're scaring me too.

GIELGUD. I feel sure there's a way –

CRONYN. If Dick was to thrust it through, hold the thrust, I will use the time to step across to the left. I will place it between arm and chest, I will tumble out.

BURTON. A tiny bit 'school play', isn't it?

CRONYN. I thank you for your support.

BURTON. I'm supposed to just hold the thrust?

CRONYN. I believe in you, kid, you can take them with you.

There's laughter.

GIELGUD. We'll need longer coats. So we don't see Hume's feet, Jessica...

JESSICA. Consider it done.

BURTON. You think this is a good idea?

GIELGUD. I think it's worth trying. If you're game…

> BURTON *nods. Unsure. They're all on their best behaviour here.*

> Can we try it from 'He will come straight'? Perhaps, let's have Eileen here and Hume over here. Off we go.

CRONYN.
> He will come straight. Look you lay home to him.
> Tell him his pranks have been too broad to bear with,
> And that your grace hath screened and stood between
> Much heat and him. I'll sconce me even here.
> Pray you, be round with him.

HERLIE.
> I'll warrant you, fear me not.

BURTON (*within*).
> Mother, mother, mother!

HERLIE.
> Withdraw, I hear him coming.

> CRONYN *hides behind the cloak rack.*

BURTON.
> Now, mother, what's the matter?

HERLIE.
> Hamlet, thou hast thy father much offended.

BURTON
> Mother, you have my father much offended.

HERLIE.
> Come, come, you answer with an idle tongue.

BURTON.
> Go, go, you question with a wicked tongue.

HERLIE.
> Why, how now, Hamlet!

BURTON.
> What's the matter now?

HERLIE.
> Have you forgot me?

BURTON.
> No, by the rood, not so:
> You are the Queen, your husband's brother's wife,
> And – would it were not so! – you are my mother.

There's a silence as these words sink in. GIELGUD *smiles.*

HERLIE.
> Nay, then, I'll set those to you that can speak.

BURTON.
> Come, come, and sit you down; you shall not budge.
> You go not till I set you up a glass
> Where you may see the inmost part of you.

HERLIE.
> What wilt thou do? Thou wilt not murder me?
> Help, ho!

CRONYN.
> What, ho! Help!

BURTON *draws out a sword.*

BURTON.
> How now! a rat? Dead, for a ducat, dead!

HERLIE.
> No!

BURTON *thrusts the sword through the coats.*

CRONYN (*from behind the rack*).
> O, I am slain!

HERLIE.
> O me, what hast thou done?

BURTON.
> Nay, I know not. Is it the King?

HERLIE.

O, what a rash and bloody deed is this!

BURTON.

A bloody deed! Almost as bad, good mother,
As kill a King, and marry with his brother.

HERLIE.

As kill a King!

BURTON.

Ay, lady, it was my word.

He pushes through the coats and finds CRONYN. *He gasps
in horror.*

Thou wretched, rash, intruding fool –

GIELGUD. Good. A good first draft.

CRONYN (*indicating the rack hopefully*). I thought that
worked rather well.

GIELGUD. Yes.

Beat. GIELGUD *has a note and he isn't sure how to give it.*

Dick – just a small thought. The line 'Is it the King?' I think
it might need a little more energy. 'Have I done it? Have
I killed the filthy pig?'

BURTON. He's a gentle man, John. He doesn't want to kill
anyone.

GIELGUD. That is one point of view, the other is that you hate
the King. You're an avenger. You must –

BURTON. No. No. It's 'Oh God, have I done what I always
feared I'd do?'

Beat.

GIELGUD. Dear boy, we need to get the audience out of their
seats – and as we're leaving the diffidence aside and
focusing on the fighter quality of your Hamlet –

BURTON. No one's leaving the diffidence aside. We need to
tell the truth –

GIELGUD. But this can be the truth.

BURTON. What do you want, John? You want anxiety, fear, guilt and triumph all at once – you may be able to play that, I cannot.

GIELGUD. It is not what I can play and you can't –

BURTON. Thrills and upswings are always desirable – but Hamlet is a gentle man –

GIELGUD. Then why is he thrusting his sword into a closet?

BURTON. He's agitated.

GIELGUD. It is a large agitation – is it not? To thrust a sword into a closet without knowing what lurks there? He has had many opportunities to kill Claudius, he has taken none of them – but in his mother's own room he kills a wardrobe? Surely this is a scene which suits your Hamlet best?

There's silence.

BURTON. I don't know who you think my Hamlet *is*, but what you're saying is not consistent with the Hamlet I'm trying to *play*. Which is, of course, the Hamlet that is written. Who is a gentle man.

GIELGUD *knows this moment will blow up if he continues. He pulls back.*

GIELGUD. Yes, of course, let's continue with – let's continue with – your idea –

Beat. But he can't let it go.

The reason why you can't remember the speech is because it isn't there. Titus doesn't even chop his own hand, Aaron the Moor does it. Titus gives no great speech, simply gives the axe to Aaron and says 'Come hither Aaron. I'll deceive them both; Lend me thy hand, and I will give thee mine.' So I don't know which speech of Sir Laurence Olivier's you are remembering, but it was not that one.

He clearly needed to let that out. But now it's let out it makes no difference.

BURTON. Yes, I must have been mistaken. I am a silly lump. I will aim for more accuracy in my anecdotes in future.

Beat. There's acid here again.

But I'm right about 'Is it the King?' For my Hamlet. I mean.

GIELGUD *knows he's been defeated.*

GIELGUD. Yes. You undoubtedly are. Let's try it again. From the top.

Scene Three

Day Seventeen – 'Observe His Inclination in Yourself'

GIELGUD*'s hotel room.*

GIELGUD. Do sit down, you're making me feel quite disquieted.

McHAFFIE. Nice room.

GIELGUD. Thank you.

Beat.

There's no need to look so uncomfortable. If you wish to leave, you can.

McHAFFIE. I think my shoes might have dirt on them.

GIELGUD. You're frightened of the carpet? Of course you are. How lovely.

McHAFFIE. I'm not frightened of it.

GIELGUD. The question is then – should you take your shoes off or are your socks in a worse state?

McHAFFIE. Sorry?

GIELGUD. I believe I have some hotel slippers. Or perhaps you can just be barefoot. The carpet is a nice one to be bare with. How bad are one's feet?

McHAFFIE. You say don't be uncomfortable and you're making me uncomfortable.

GIELGUD. I am. I apologise. Nerves perhaps.

McHAFFIE. No need to be nervous. You paid for it. I'm good to my word. Consider it a contract. I won't hurt you. I'm not one of those guys.

GIELGUD. Perhaps it is my actions I'm nervous of.

McHAFFIE. You want to hurt me? You can. For more.

GIELGUD. Good grief no.

McHAFFIE. Then what do you want me to do?

GIELGUD. Did anyone notice? Do you think? Us coming in?

McHAFFIE. No.

Beat.

Don't think I've ever had an Englishman before.

GIELGUD. How transatlantic for you.

McHAFFIE. I can blow you, or you can fuck me. Like I say, I don't really want to fuck you. Or I can use my hand.

GIELGUD. Oh, how wonderful it's a multiple choice.

McHAFFIE. You want me to take my clothes off?

GIELGUD. No, thank you. That'd spoil the surprise.

Beat.

A drink?

McHAFFIE. I don't have long, to be honest with you.

GIELGUD *ignores him as he pours himself a drink.*

GIELGUD. One of your policeman stopped me – must be the day before yesterday – I'd dropped my umbrella and he said 'Hey, fairy, you dropped your wand.' I can't even think what I must have been wearing. So much easier, it feels, to be spotted here than it is back home. Perhaps all Englishman are fairies here.

McHAFFIE. You say anything back?

GIELGUD. Of course I did, I retrieved my umbrella, pointed it at him and said 'Vanish.'

McHAFFIE *grins*.

McHAFFIE. That's pretty funny.

GIELGUD. Could he have done something rotten to me for it?

McHAFFIE. If he wanted to. They're quite relaxed unless they catch you at it.

GIELGUD. You've been caught a few times?

McHAFFIE. Perils of the job. You?

GIELGUD. Just the once.

Beat. We hear the pain of that 'once'.

Have you been safe? Do you feel safe here?

Beat.

You're rather beautiful, you know that?

McHAFFIE. You don't want to fuck me at all, do you?

GIELGUD. I'm sorry, I'm afraid I love another.

McHAFFIE. So why am I up here?

GIELGUD. I just wanted to do something reckless.

McHAFFIE. You feel better now you have?

GIELGUD. Not especially.

Beat. McHAFFIE *comes and sits beside him.*

McHAFFIE. What's his name?

GIELGUD. Martin.

McHAFFIE. He's at home?

GIELGUD. Yes.

McHAFFIE. How long you been together?

GIELGUD. Two years. As my professional life has crumbled my personal life has grown. He's the first I've ever – truly – trusted myself with.

McHAFFIE. How old are you?

GIELGUD. Let's have fun. Why don't you guess.

McHAFFIE. Sixty?

GIELGUD winces.

GIELGUD. How clever of you. Yes, I'm sixty years old.

McHAFFIE. You're still a good-looking man, you know that?

GIELGUD. I don't need therapy from you.

McHAFFIE. You are.

GIELGUD. Very charming of you to say, but you have no idea how damning the 'still' addition is in that sentence.

McHAFFIE. You were really good-looking once, huh?

GIELGUD. I was.

McHAFFIE. Then – the hair – always hard to lose the hair…

GIELGUD. Luckily I work in a profession where wigs are encouraged.

McHAFFIE. I knew you were an actor. This hotel always gets the fag actors.

Beat.

Sixty years old and you've only just found love. There's tragedy in that.

GIELGUD. There's tragedy in all of us.

McHAFFIE. I hope I get luckier.

GIELGUD. I hope so too. You should probably go. Use my time on the clock to have a drink in the hotel bar or grab some of that fabulous pizza you people like so much.

McHAFFIE. Hold me.

GIELGUD. I'm fine.

McHAFFIE. Hold me. You'll like it.

Beat. McHAFFIE *approaches him.*

I'm not leaving till you give me a cuddle, sir.

GIELGUD. A cuddle. What a word for a man like you to use.

McHAFFIE. We all got mothers.

GIELGUD *stands, and then lets himself be gently held.*

GIELGUD. Delightful.

McHAFFIE. You're not trying hard enough.

GIELGUD *melts slightly.*

There you go. There you go. That's the way.

GIELGUD *starts sobbing.*

GIELGUD. I'm sorry. How awful. I can't help it. I was born with my bladder too close to my eyes. One blink and it comes out.

He looks at him.

Not self-pity you understand, merely gratitude for your kindness.

McHAFFIE. Okay now. Okay. Okay. I got you. Okay.

Scene Four

Day Nineteen – 'Let Me Be Cruel'

BURTON *is pacing his room like a lion. He is in his vest and briefs. He is talking to himself, murmuring rather than acting, as he goes over his lines.*

BURTON.
Now might I do it pat, now he is a-praying.
And now I'll do't, and so he goes to heaven.
And so am I revenged. That would be scanned.
A villain kills my father; and for that
I, his sole son, do this same villain send –

There is a ring on the doorbell.

BURTON *doesn't move to answer it. There is another ring.*

TAYLOR *walks past in her underwear to answer it.*

BURTON. No.

TAYLOR. Yes.

BURTON. Put some clothes on at least.

TAYLOR. Says he.

BURTON. I don't threaten tumescence in the visitor in quite the same way.

TAYLOR. You underestimate yourself. And our visitors.

BURTON. What did we drink last night?

TAYLOR. You know, that is how you should play Hamlet, far more authentic for you to be in your underwear half the time.

BURTON. Get thee to a nunnery.

TAYLOR. Oh, darling, could you imagine?

There is another doorbell.

BURTON. What did we drink last night?

TAYLOR. If you can't remember then why would I?

TAYLOR *answers the door to a flustered* REDFIELD.

REDFIELD. I'm sorry, I interrupted –

TAYLOR. If you did, we wouldn't have answered. I'll put some clothes on. Find a pill.

She exits.

BURTON. She's feeling insecure I think. Wanted to accost a stranger.

REDFIELD. Did she… did I…

BURTON. Either that or she's hungover and doesn't care. You did exactly right. You were startled and awestruck. Why are you here?

REDFIELD. You invited me…

BURTON. Did I?

REDFIELD. You wanted to run the – do a line-run…

BURTON. I may have phoned you sloshed. I'm sorry.

REDFIELD. Then I will leave you be.

BURTON. No. No. You're very welcome. Shall I call down for more coffee?

REDFIELD. No.

BURTON. Hold steady, I'll put some trousers on.

He makes to exit.

REDFIELD. I wanted to play Laertes.

BURTON looks up.

He said it didn't fit with his conception of how you were to play it. 'You see, we are doing the play in rehearsal clothes and without a formal set. I must force myself to cast according to type. I want a modern, delinquent quality from Laertes. Frightfully young.'

BURTON. That is a quite an impressive impression.

REDFIELD. 'Would you,' he said to me 'consider reading Guildenstern for me? Make him rather a booby? Perhaps find a bit of comedy from him at last. I must not have boys or fops in these roles. Hamlet must be played as thirty-five, because of Richard Burton, and you must be contemporaries of his. Do you see?'

BURTON. You have a good memory.

REDFIELD. It's not word for word, but it's – uh – I remember what he said – it was my first time meeting him and I try to remember when talking to the greats.

BURTON. I must watch what I say then.

REDFIELD. You are not a –

BURTON. I was making a joke, I know I'm not a great. I must find my trousers.

REDFIELD. The joke was predicated on the possibility of greatness though. It wouldn't mean the same coming from me. And I couldn't agree more about the trousers.

BURTON. You think you're the first to say that? Richard Burton, 'nearly great'. Not quite. But almost. Why do you think I'm here? Trying to play Hamlet?

REDFIELD. Ego.

BURTON. Ouch.

TAYLOR *appears back into the room, she's in a dress and has quickly put some eye make-up on.*

REDFIELD. If a man – in fury – hacking at a piece of wood – constructs thereby the image of a cow – can it be beautiful?

BURTON. Joyce.

REDFIELD. Is it? I thought it was E. M. Forster.

BURTON. *Portrait of the Artist as a Young Man.*

REDFIELD. Goodness. Is that right?

BURTON. I respect books. Confounding question, isn't it? Is a cow beautiful? And does the manner in which art is made matter?

REDFIELD. Marlon Brando is a friend of mine.

BURTON. Yes, you like famous people, I can see that about you.

REDFIELD. His *Streetcar* – onstage – the film is barely a shadow of it – was extraordinary –

BURTON. I am not Marlon Brando.

REDFIELD. No, you have a modicum more respect for yourself. You know what he's made since *Waterfront*?

BURTON. *Guys and Dolls*, wasn't it? That was awful. Why sing when you can't?

TAYLOR. *Teahouse of the August Moon, Sayonara, Young Lions, Fugitive Kind, One-Eyed Jacks, Mutiny on the Bounty* and *Guys and Dolls.*

They both look at TAYLOR, *surprised by this.*

BURTON. You keep a close eye on him then?

TAYLOR. I'm interested in what he's doing wrong. We eat from the same plate. He has control of his choices as I do of mine. Those are the actors I need watch. And William is right, Marlon has cost everyone money and done no good with it. A mistake in every book. Should I leave you be?

BURTON. No, he's breaking me down to size, you deserve to hear it.

REDFIELD. All were good scripts, I read some of them.

TAYLOR. I did too, some misguided but good.

REDFIELD. All he went into with such strong feeling. All he destroyed.

Beat.

BURTON. As I've destroyed this.

REDFIELD. Not yet. But the question of the cow persists…

BURTON. You're asking the question whether the fact that we have had such a terrible process should or will impact on what we've made…

REDFIELD. I thought this was an opportunity to be in something that lives for all time. That's all I want. To touch that. That greatness.

He walks back toward the door.

BURTON. Did I invite you or is this an intervention of some kind?

REDFIELD. Now's not the time to run lines. I hope you understand. I hope you feel it needed saying.

BURTON. He's also not a good director.

REDFIELD. They say actors are sponges, well, directors are too – but a different kind. We squeeze everything out of them we can.

He exits.

TAYLOR. What a darling man.

BURTON. I either need a drink or a slap and I can't decide which.

TAYLOR *kisses him gently on the lips.*

TAYLOR. I believe you married me because I'm quite prepared to give you both.

Scene Five

Day Twenty-One – 'Enter the Ghost'

HERLIE *stands centre-stage. She has a quiet power to her grief.*

HERLIE.
There is a willow grows aslant a brook,
That shows his hoar leaves in the glassy stream.
There with fantastic garlands did she come
Of crowflowers, nettles, daisies, and long purples,
That liberal shepherds give a grosser name,
But our cold maids do dead men's fingers call them.
There, on the pendent boughs her coronet weeds
Clamb'ring to hang, an envious sliver broke,
When down her weedy trophies and herself
Fell in the weeping brook. Her clothes spread wide,
And mermaid-like, awhile they bore her up,
Which time she chanted snatches of old tunes
As one incapable of her own distress,
Or like a creature native and indued
Unto that element: but long it could not be
Till that her garments, heavy with their drink,
Pulled the poor wretch from her melodious lay
To muddy death.

LAERTES.
Alas then, she is drowned?

HERLIE.
Drowned, drowned.

LAERTES.
    Too much of water hast thou, poor Ophelia,
    And therefore I forbid my tears.

GIELGUD. Lovely, Eileen, you've really caught the simplicity
    since our last rehearsal, very telling, can't say I miss
    Claudius's last lines at all –

DRAKE. Nor I.

GIELGUD. Good. Now let's work on the transition to Act Four,
    Scene Eight if we might…

BURTON. Actually. Could we have the room?

    BURTON *has appeared inconspicuously in the background.*

GIELGUD. Ah, King Richard. I did not notice you.

BURTON. I was lurking. That was beautiful, Eileen.

HERLIE. Thank you.

BURTON. Would you all mind? I fear I must talk to Sir John
    alone and – time is pressing…

HERLIE. Not at all.

    They clear the room.

    They do so in silence.

    We realise these two titanic souls are finally about to meet.

GIELGUD. So – how might we – uh – how might I – what do
    you require?

BURTON. You're frightened I'm going to fire you, aren't you?

GIELGUD. I would.

BURTON. Or – you might try and fire me.

GIELGUD. Who wants to be the man who fired Dick Burton?

BURTON. Who wants to be the man who fired Sir John Gielgud?

    There's a silence.

GIELGUD. So you're here to talk about process? Or…

BURTON. To be or not to be.

GIELGUD. Ahhh, the question. For you or the character? For the whole project perhaps?

BURTON. Why say it?

GIELGUD *looks at him carefully.*

GIELGUD. There are many ways of reading it.

BURTON. How do you read it?

GIELGUD. If it were my Hamlet I'd be battling with the question as to whether I'm strong enough for what's ahead. I'd be considering my responsibility to myself and my country. I could bring civil war with this action. But, I repeat, this is not my Hamlet...

BURTON. I think my Hamlet is weighing up similar, whether he will fight for his father or slit his own throat –

GIELGUD. Dear boy, have you considered, could it be – that your Hamlet does not like his father.

BURTON *looks at* GIELGUD, *surprised.*

BURTON. This whole play is about a man who loves his father –

GIELGUD. He was a cuckold. He was a weak man. You loved him, but he never gave you what you truly wanted in a King. Maybe he was an adequate father, maybe he loved you, but he's not the King you'd be, you wanted more, better, and now you must risk everything to fight for him?

BURTON *starts to get excited.*

BURTON. That is his dilemma – that's the centre of the play – whether Hamlet should fight for a man – *destroy a kingdom* for a man – he neither liked nor respected? You've never said this before.

GIELGUD. I'd never thought it before you posed the question. Take that through the play and you will take the whole audience with you. This is how we do it. Your Hamlet is a bugle, ready with sword whenever required. It is not self-conviction he lacks, it is the reason to fight at all.

GIELGUD *looks at* BURTON, *and then he starts to shed his skin.*

My father married into the Terrys, you know. You imagine marrying into that lineage? Of course you can, look who you married –

BURTON. True enough.

GIELGUD. A stockbroker. Loved theatre, loved it, but also loved museums – oh – the pain of that – being dragged from one museum to another. He wanted me to be an architect. He understood my heritage, admired it, but did not want me to follow it. The bargain I made with him was that if I wasn't able to be self-supporting by the age of twenty-five, I would take an office job. Of course, by twenty-five –

BURTON. You were playing Hamlet.

GIELGUD *nods.*

GIELGUD. Not sure he ever knew I was homosexual. Often wonder what he would have thought of that. But whilst I wonder, I also can't say I greatly care either way and ay, there's the rub. He was kind, he was gentle, he was interesting on occasion, but he was deeply average. Not the man I wanted to grow into. I was indifferent to him. But I loved him.

BURTON. I hated my father.

GIELGUD. Did you?

BURTON. My mother died when I was two years old and he was all that I had.

GIELGUD. He didn't live up to that?

BURTON. From the pit to the pub and then back again. Twelve-pints-a-day man. Damn anyone who got in the way of that. He gave me to my sister. Deposited me. She did the best she could. She loved me.

Beat.

My father was a bully, a drunk and he left me.

GIELGUD. What a fool he was to do so.

BURTON *nods. But he can't quite look at* GIELGUD. *His soul is starting to be exposed too.*

The motive and the cue. Hamlet's own words. The motive is the spine of a role – the intellect and the reason – the cue is the passion – the inner switch which ignites the heart. We can colour ourselves with limps and canes, with green umbrellas and purple suits, but we cannot escape the motive and the cue.

There's a profound silence.

Why do you do theatre? You could be earning much better money elsewhere, and I know you do like money. And I know you like relaxing too. You gave up five hundred thousand, perhaps more, to crawl into a hair shirt. Why? What for?

BURTON. You've asked me that question before –

GIELGUD. I'm not sure you answered it.

BURTON. I think I like the rigour of it –

GIELGUD. No.

BURTON. The comradeship –

GIELGUD. Wrong again.

BURTON. It feels like you have an answer ready prepared –

GIELGUD. Am I so see-through?

BURTON. I have the patience for it. Tell me my answer –

GIELGUD. You like the art. That relationship between the audience and the stage – that moment of conversation – theatre is thinking – pure thought – collective imagination yes, but also just – I don't think there is any other art form in the world where minds meet so beautifully. One thousand people, sat together, in communion with what's in front of them.

BURTON. So I'm expected to be a priest now?

GIELGUD. The actor and the character. Wasn't that where we started? How you cannot separate them. The audience has been told this story a thousand times – *Hamlet*, oh, how dull, everyone dies, but one must go to see it, rattle our jewellery,

someone famous is in it you know – but they've never heard
you tell it, and your pain and your suffering makes it yours.
And that means they are delighted by discovering it anew.
Because you have remade it for them. You are going to hold
them in your thoughts. Your actions. Your deeds. Your Hamlet.

BURTON. Powerful words –

GIELGUD. But don't you believe them?

BURTON *says nothing, but it's clear he's taken.*

Try it for me.

BURTON. Which?

GIELGUD. Tell me why you're unsure whether your father is
worth this.

BURTON *looks at him and then nods.*

BURTON.
To be, or not to be, that is the question:
Whether 'tis nobler in the mind to suffer
The slings and arrows of outrageous fortune,
Or to take arms against a sea of troubles
And by opposing end them. To die, to sleep –
No more – and by a sleep to say we end
The heartache and the thousand natural shocks
That flesh is heir to – 'tis a consummation
Devoutly to be wished. To die, to sleep.
To sleep, perchance to dream – ay, there's the rub.
For in that sleep of death what dreams may come,
When we have shuffled off this mortal coil,
Must give us pause – there's the respect
That makes calamity of so long life.
For who would bear the whips and scorns of time,
Th'oppressor's wrong, the proud man's contumely,
The pangs of despised love, the law's delay,
The insolence of office and the spurns
That patient merit of th'unworthy takes,
When he himself might his quietus make
With a bare bodkin?

There's a silence. BURTON *is held. Powerful. Strong.*

Who would fardels bear,
To grunt and sweat under a weary life,
But that the dread of something after death,
The undiscovered country from whose bourn
No traveller returns, puzzles the will,
And makes us rather bear those ills we have
Than fly to others that we know not of?
Thus conscience does make cowards of us all,
And thus the native hue of resolution
Is sicklied o'er with the pale cast of thought,
And enterprises of great pitch and moment
With this regard their currents turn awry,
And lose the name of action.

There's a silence.

BURTON *stands swaying, thoroughly daunted but unleashed by the truth of what he's just found.*

GIELGUD. And *that* is a Hamlet I have never seen.

Scene Six

Day Twenty-Five – 'The Table of My Memory'

The champagne corks pop to cheers.

BURTON. I'm making a bloody speech, I don't care what you fools say.

CRONYN. You're wrong, Dick, 'tis I that will make the speech.

BURTON. The final rehearsal. The gun has been cocked. I must.

HERLIE. No, no, I shall make the speech in the style of Hume.

MILLI. Now this I'd like to see.

REDFIELD. I'm celebrating leaving that damn rehearsal room is what I'm celebrating –

HERLIE. 'As my wife Jessica – Tandy if you didn't know, my wife is Jessica Tandy…'

There's laughter.

CRONYN. I'd say no such thing. Outrageous.

TAYLOR. You do mention her a lot. I think it's sweet.

CRONYN. Says the woman who can't stop talking about her –
husband*s* –

There's laughter.

TAYLOR. Now now, Hume –

BURTON. Destroy him. Please.

TAYLOR. Too easy surely.

HERLIE. Let's have a competition. Throw rotten eggs at Hume
and see which one disrupts him best –

EVANS. I will go first.

DRAKE. Nonsense, I will go first.

CRONYN. You know, there was a time when I commanded
respect in a rehearsal room –

REDFIELD. Really? And I thought myself a student of theatre.

There are ooohs from around the room.

CRONYN. Who broke Redfield? He used to be so nice.

REDFIELD. Never nice. Just watching. Like a snake. Waiting
for the moment to attack.

CRONYN. If I *were* to make a speech, you know what I'd say?
What I like about actors…

DRAKE. There is nothing to like about actors.

CRONYN. I believe you will not meet a more tough-gutted and
realistic group of people in the world. The theatre's
guarantee of employment is nil, the theatre's competition is
savage, the theatre's employers are gamblers. Actors know
that if the play fails, Armageddon is upon them – but they
will survive. Show me a working actor and I will show you
a man – or woman – with a cement stomach.

HERLIE *(as Hume)*. And my wife's stomach is the best in the
business.

There's cheering.

CRONYN. So we ran at three hours thirteen today –

YOUNG (*as Gielgud*). 'With at least ten minutes left to lose.'

CRONYN. And the play made sense, indeed it was rather moving, there was something quite inevitable about the whole thing – with a Prince who was a – Prince.

He nods to BURTON *who takes it with pleasure.*

VOSKOVEC. Hear hear.

CRONYN. In fact, you were all marvellous. Even you, Eileen.

HERLIE. Oh please.

There's applause.

TAYLOR. Perhaps I can say something also?

REDFIELD. You simply must. It's inevitable.

There's laughter.

TAYLOR. I'm going to stand on a table now – this table – but none of you are allowed to look up my skirt.

There's laughter. She clambers up.

And my speech – is about this man here.

Pause.

What drugs might help Richard relax on his first performance?

There's cheers.

BURTON. I'm not going anywhere near your cabinet of hell.

TAYLOR. Oh come now, theatre actors are the most nervous creatures I've ever come across…

REDFIELD. Perhaps Dexamyl? It's got me through some tough spots now and then. Can dry the mouth though…

TAYLOR. Dexamyl it is.

CRONYN. You really dose before a show?

GIELGUD. How surprising, I need only masturbate and I'm quite ready.

They all turn. GIELGUD *has entered surreptitiously.*

The doorman let me past. I hope that's alright. I was invited.

TAYLOR. You're very welcome. We were just discussing nervousness.

GIELGUD. Oh, I despise them. Nerves. Still, they sometimes make one do wonderful things. I always think.

There's a silence.

I've made everyone uncomfortable, and you were having such fun before.

CRONYN. Sir John, tell us about those early years at the Vic.

GIELGUD. Oh Hume. How sweet. But I'm not sure even a question-and-answer can save me now – I'll leave.

REDFIELD. I'd like to know.

TAYLOR. We'd all like to know. It's all our history and only you lived it.

GIELGUD. History is for old people. Stay young and avoid it.

BURTON. In a little over two years at The Old Vic he played most of the Shakespeare cannon. Romeo, Antonio, Richard II, Oberon, Mark Antony, Orlando, Macbeth –

HERLIE. Oh Jesus. Hume – turn around three times and touch the floor with your tongue.

BURTON. Hotspur, Prospero, Benedick, Lear and Hamlet. Of course. Over four hundred times, at the Vic and in the West End. But truthfully, he made his mark on every one of those characters, and left his contemporaries floundering in his wake.

There's a pause. GIELGUD *is desperately moved.*

GIELGUD. You're – uh – you – that's very kind to remember all – uh. Performances 'writ in water' as Tyrone Guthrie once said. It wasn't like that. We simply made everything we could, tumbling from one production to the next, whilst Lilian Baylis grilled bacon in the wings.

TAYLOR. Who is this woman and why haven't I heard of her?

GIELGUD. A patron of the arts who was quite quite mad. And quite quite wonderful. And she really liked bacon. But – enough of looking backwards, we should all look forwards. Who has had a good obscene phone call we can talk of?

HERLIE. Jesus!

GIELGUD. I keep trying to talk Martin into one, but then the dogs interfere and we're sunk.

BURTON. I've had one.

TAYLOR. Not with me.

BURTON. Before you.

TAYLOR. There's no before me.

BURTON. How fascinating. There's four husbands before me.

There's laughter.

TAYLOR. He's just as wicked when we're alone, you know…

REDFIELD. Now that's an obscene phone call I'd like to be on.

There's silence.

Between you and him, I mean. Just to listen. For the laugh of it.

TAYLOR. Give me your phone number and we shall make it happen.

There's laughter.

But there'll be no laughter you understand.

REDFIELD. Oh dear. I didn't mean…

HERLIE. You did and you would. Heck, I'm playing his mother and I would if I could.

GIELGUD. That is what we'll make together once this is over. A giant obscene phone call, and we'll put William here centre-stage and he won't be allowed to say a word.

BURTON. And all our voices will be recorded like your Ghost.

CRONYN. So none of us need turn up and act every night?
This sounds glorious.

GIELGUD. We'll use and abuse our pocket books and get a cast
the likes of which Broadway has never seen.

REDFIELD. I get top billing. I get top billing.

HERLIE. I'll take no billing at all if I get a cut of box office.

TAYLOR. It'll be a tremendous scandal.

CRONYN. And a glory for years to come.

GIELGUD. To Broadway.

He raises a glass.

COMPANY. To Broadway.

He raises it again.

GIELGUD. To theatre.

COMPANY. To theatre.

He raises it again.

GIELGUD. To Uncle Will.

COMPANY. To Uncle Will.

BURTON *raises a glass.*

BURTON. To Sir John Gielgud.

COMPANY. To Sir John Gielgud.

GIELGUD. Don't be so ridiculous.

CRONYN. For he's a jolly good fellow.

COMPANY. For he's a jolly good fellow.

GIELGUD. You're all awful.

COMPANY. For he's a jolly good felloooooooow.
And so say all of us.

Scene Seven

First Preview – 'Remember Me'

TAYLOR *stands alone on the stage looking out.*

TAYLOR.
Gallop apace, you fiery-footed steeds,
Towards Phoebus' lodging: such a wagoner
As Phaethon would whip you to the west,
And bring in cloudy night immediately.
Spread thy close curtain, love-performing night,
That runaway's eyes may wink and Romeo
Leap to these arms, untalk'd of and unseen.

She enjoys the words and finishes with a smile.

She takes in the room. She repeats a few words under her breath as if trying to gather a better performance. She searches for, as always, perfection.

GIELGUD. Now what on earth are you doing here?

TAYLOR turns, for a moment anxious – did he hear her? She recomposes herself.

TAYLOR. Dick told me the stage was clear. I thought I'd take a moment.

GIELGUD. Who would you give?

TAYLOR. Oh, probably Hamlet.

GIELGUD smiles.

I'd love to have seen yours.

GIELGUD. It was an albatross for a while, you know. The part I was born for. It rather meant people struggled to see me as anything else. My best was in 1929. Can you imagine doing your best work at twenty-five?

TAYLOR. Can you imagine doing it at twelve?

They smile at each other in mutual admiration.

GIELGUD. It was the finest of times. I remember just wallowing in pleasure in the bath after every show. I had the whole theatre in my hand. I could feel it. And now all people remember is his... because of the damn film.

TAYLOR. Damn films.

GIELGUD. Larry played Hamlet only once you know – in London at least, then once at Elsinore and then the – film. But on the stage... just once. Michael Redgrave was his Laertes, dear Vanessa was born during the engagement. 1937. It was a good production, but as another actor – I shan't name him – discretion – it wasn't Michael – said 'It was the finest performance of Hotspur that I have ever seen.'

TAYLOR hoots.

TAYLOR. I used to think film actors were savage but we've nothing on you lot.

GIELGUD. You're rather charming, Miss Taylor. And personally, I think you'd give a wonderful Juliet...

TAYLOR. No.

GIELGUD. Lady Macbeth then. There's a part in it for your husband too, that he'd be particularly well suited to.

TAYLOR. I thought we didn't use that name in a theatre. Brought curses, et cetera.

GIELGUD. Ahh, we all carry curses.

Beat.

TAYLOR. Where will you sit, for the first show?

GIELGUD. I will sit up high. So I can watch the audience. After which, I must leave, I have a friend ill at home – Bernie –

TAYLOR. You're leaving?

GIELGUD. For a moment. I must get back to him.

TAYLOR. A special friend?

GIELGUD. All friends are special, Miss Taylor. But no, not special in the way you imply. But important. An ally. And I want to be close to my allies. Life has taught me that much.

Besides, my work is done, Richard won't listen to me any more and – not that he ever quite did – a good fight though, one does enjoy a good fight.

TAYLOR. Did you? Enjoy it?

GIELGUD. I'm never quite sure what I feel most of the time. Unless I'm onstage that is, when I have such clarity –

TAYLOR. Michael – Wilding always used to say –

GIELGUD. I know Michael Wilding! How delightful! Such a charming man, I can't imagine how he got mixed up with all those dreadful tarts. How do you – ?

TAYLOR. I was one of the dreadful tarts.

GIELGUD looks at her a moment, unabashed.

GIELGUD. Of course you were.

TAYLOR takes his arm.

TAYLOR. Michael always used to say to me. When I was wobbling. You are going to be fine you know. And I really do believe it. In your respect especially.

Beat. Those are words with an impact.

It's the same as the movies, there'll be a moment, when the world adjusts, and then – just like that – you'll be treasured again, just like you should be.

There's a silence.

A stillness.

The words work their way through him.

GIELGUD. I do hope you're right.

He walks on through the theatre, through the auditorium, and out.

But my only remaining ambition is to do an underwear advertisement which would start with me – sat in my intimates – saying 'At my time of life, all is quiet on the Y-front.'

TAYLOR *laughs as she watches him go.*

And then BURTON *enters behind her.*

BURTON. Is that him going? John. Sir JOHN. John. Oh, he mustn't be able to hear. Shall I chase after him?

TAYLOR. No, darling, protect your knees for another time.

He looks at his wife.

BURTON. Do you think I'm ready? For tonight?

TAYLOR. Do you?

BURTON. Not at all.

BURTON *looks at her and smiles.*

TAYLOR. Give me a glimpse.

BURTON. No.

TAYLOR. Give me your 'to be or not to be'.

BURTON. Never.

She kisses him.

TAYLOR. Then fuck me on your stage. As quickly as you can manage. I'm not wearing knickers.

BURTON. No.

He grins.

You're not wearing knickers?

TAYLOR. I speak the truth. And I love you.

BURTON. She finally finds me attractive.

TAYLOR. That's why you like me, because I get to choose.

BURTON. Go on. Clear off. The actors will be down for warm-up in a moment.

TAYLOR. I came here for you, remember that. I turned down millions of dollars – sumptuous roles – to be here for you.

BURTON. I will return your gift in droves.

TAYLOR. I'm not sure that's true. But I know what it is to have people dance around me and, for once, I was happy to dance around you.

She kisses him again and then picks up her things and exits.
BURTON *looks around the theatre.*

BURTON. Lizzie. Have I behaved badly?

TAYLOR. Darling, you've never done anything but.

And she's gone.

BURTON *looks out. He adjusts himself.*

He paces. He tries to control himself.

But it's hard.

GIELGUD. Ah. I interrupted a private moment. I rather forgot my hat you see…

GIELGUD *is standing at the back of the stalls, he walks forward.*

And they stand together.

I do like first nights. The discovery of what's ahead.

BURTON. I'm mostly terrified.

GIELGUD. Envious. I'm envious. Terrible quality in a director I suspect.

BURTON. You'd still want to do it again?

GIELGUD. With every inch of my burning soul. But time is against me. It's your time now.

Beat. BURTON *smiles.*

BURTON. Any last words?

GIELGUD. A lesson for you from an old man, never try to have the last word. It's frightfully boring. Let them speak first and last. And then take all the words in between.

BURTON *smiles.*

BURTON. This can be my Hamlet?

GIELGUD *shows his wound.*

GIELGUD. I heard you just now, when you called for me, when I was leaving the theatre, and I couldn't quite face you and then I thought I must – bravery demands it, and theatre is bravery, so I returned – my hat is – elsewhere.

BURTON. If I have offended you – caused you pain – I'm sorry –

GIELGUD. Dear boy, it *is your Hamlet.* And I've done all I can for you now. You must forget about me. The play is yours. From now on, everything is up to you, the audience and Uncle Will.

He leans in and kisses BURTON *on the cheek.*

Go well.

He exits again.

BURTON *is left.*

He steps forward.

He becomes a Prince.

He takes a deep breath.

Curtain.

Other Titles in this Series

www.nickhernbooks.co.uk

facebook.com/nickhernbooks

twitter.com/nickhernbooks